# Oradour
**Soldiers of Shame**

# Oradour
## Soldiers of Shame

*Roy Haines*

Copyright © 2025 Roy Haines

All rights reserved. No part of this publication may be reproduced or transmitted in any form or by any means, electronic or mechanical including photocopying, recording or any information storage or retrieval system, without prior permission in writing from the publishers.

The right of Roy Haines to be identified as the author of this work has been asserted by him in accordance with the Copyright, Designs and Patents Act 1988

First published in the United Kingdom in 2025 by
The Choir Press

ISBN 978-1-78963-565-2

# Preface

"NOBODY LIVES HERE NOW" ... THESE WERE THE words of Lord Olivier when he began his narration of 'The World at War', probably the most authoritative televised account of the Second World War. The story of the murders and the destruction that took place at Oradour-sur-Glane was chosen for the introductory and closing episodes of the series because it is a tragic symbol of the mindless cruelty that mankind may resort to during warfare. The decision by the French to preserve the village as it was immediately after the massacre remains controversial. There were initial concerns that this policy might prove to be nothing more than sensationalism or an attraction for the morbidly curious. But throughout the passing decades, Oradour's ruins have fulfilled their objective: they are stark evidence of 'Man's inhumanity to Man'. Oradour also serves as a memorial to the worst atrocity against civilians by ground troops in Western Europe during the Second World War. More significantly, it is a warning to future generations who will inevitably become involved in warfare, at some time, somewhere in this world.

*RDH*

# Oradour-sur-Glane

Stone stairways end abruptly, where
once there stood doorways
through which families lived their lives of normality...
until 'They' came killing all before them

The lifeless burnt-out rusting remains
of vehicles, from another lifetime,
litter the silent streets of this slaughtered village...
and they cry out to tell their tale

The leaning walls of buildings,
once proud, crumble with age
and the atrocities of an angry age,
past doorways lead only to rubble
and glassless windows...
frame a saddened sky

Six hundred and forty two, including
women and children, were murdered here,
their screams echo from every bullet
hole and twisted piece of metal...
But the real sadness lies in the fact
that their killers were men,
who were missing their own
families, children, and wives...

*Tom Balch*
*Soldier, writer and poet*

# Contents

| | |
|---|---:|
| Preface | 1 |
| Poem by Tom Balch | 2 |
| Foreword | 4 |
| Chapter 1: Oradour Today | 10 |
| Chapter 2: France and Germany – Historic Enemies | 17 |
| Chapter 3: Refugees | 23 |
| Chapter 4: The Soldiers | 28 |
| Chapter 5: Resistance | 37 |
| Chapter 6: Invasion | 41 |
| Chapter 7: Search Plans | 46 |
| Chapter 8: Saturday 10th June 1944 | 52 |
| *Photographs and Illustrations* | 61 |
| Chapter 9: The SS Arrive | 74 |
| Chapter 10: Carnage | 82 |
| Chapter 11: The Church | 92 |
| Chapter 12: Despair | 96 |
| Chapter 13: Survivors | 102 |
| Chapter 14: Peace? | 109 |
| Chapter 15: Time Passes | 113 |
| Chapter 16: The Bordeaux Trial | 118 |
| *Photographs and Illustrations* | 128 |
| Chapter 17: Justice? | 140 |
| Chapter 18: Barth | 144 |
| Chapter 19: Aftermath | 147 |
| Some Personal Thoughts | 151 |
| Acknowledgements | 158 |
| List of Photographs and Illustrations | 159 |
| Bibliography and Other Reading | 162 |
| The Author | 163 |

# Foreword

MY GRANDAD WAS AN INFANTRY SOLDIER WHO spent much of the Great War in the trenches of Flanders. He was a farm lad with only a functional, Edwardian education. I suspect that he had scant knowledge as to why he was expected to risk his life and to take the life of others in that complex, slaughterous war. He came from an era when society expected young men to obey the call of King and Country without question. He survived, only just, with a stomach full of shrapnel, but to my knowledge, of sound mind and with a clear conscience.

My dad was also a soldier. Just like the previous generation he obeyed the call to fight and served most of the Second World War in the jungle terrain of Burma. He told me that he despised the war and that he had been in a perpetual state of fear throughout the long four years of the Far Eastern campaign. After several years on, or close to the front line, he experienced a 'mental breakdown' and was briefly sent to a rehabilitation centre in India. He soon 'recovered' and was promptly returned to his unit, still close to the front line, where he remained for the rest of the war. Typically of his generation, it was only in his final years that he told the family how mentally traumatised he had been. He told me that he had returned to his unit from the rehabilitation centre because he had little choice ... he was a soldier and his job was to fight. But he also said that he went back because he did not want to be the one who 'let the side down'. He didn't want to be branded a coward; he did not want to be isolated from his comrades. I have no idea what mental strain it must have taken for him to control his fears and to return to his post. I have heard many times that in war, the soldier's unit becomes his 'family'; his primary concerns are for his fellow soldiers.

I too became a soldier in the 1960s. But it was different for me ... there was no war that I was aware of? I was of a comfortable generation where the carnages of the two world wars were already becoming faded memories. War was something in the movies where the brave guys fought the bad guys and won ... and as a bonus, usually got the girl! I did not obey the call ... I volunteered! It was an exciting career and it took me away from the mundane council estate existence of my youth.

I was professionally trained in soldiering and military engineering and I achieved promotion to the dazzling heights of corporal! But my heart was not set on a long military career. I served only six years, and thankfully, I did not experience any fighting. I did spend a very brief period in Belfast as the 'troubles' in Ulster were beginning to ignite. Although very much on the side-lines, I witnessed some of the 'civil unrest' and I observed hatred, fear and intolerance by people both in, and out of uniform. I also served in the Middle East, but again I experienced no conflict; just some very minor 'civil disturbances' ... but I was blissfully unaware of the bubbling undercurrent of war that was soon to engulf that eternally troubled region.

As a young soldier I was conditioned to obey the commands of my superiors; I was taught to fight and I was very much prepared to do so. I mixed with more experienced soldiers who had been 'tried and tested' in the Yemen, Borneo, Kenya and many other conflicts; several of my senior NCOs and officers had seen action in Korea and World War II. I learned that modern armies were efficient because they were commanded by an elite 'officer corps' and were well led by seasoned 'non-commissioned officers'. Loyalty, pride, morale and discipline were not just jargon ... they were the very foundation of military culture and efficiency. I had an insight into the military 'psyche'. I became aware that the soldier's way of life can be very isolated from that of civilians. 'Barrack room' humour was often brutal and insensitive; it probably needed to be in order to prepare the soldier to cope with the extremities of warfare. I remember the Padre saying "humour is a great antidote for despair". It is the soldier who sees the effects of war at first hand ... right up close! They see their fellow soldiers die; they see civilians, sometimes defenceless women and children, die!

I realised that whilst soldiers are conditioned to obey orders, they do not do so automatically; fundamentally they retain their individual character traits and strengths and weaknesses. Most orders are relatively easy to comply with, but orders like "shoot to kill" are obviously more difficult to obey. But an army cannot afford protracted moral debate in open warfare, orders on the battlefield *must* be obeyed! If a soldier is ordered to kill in battle, he probably will.

Post-traumatic stress disorder is a relatively modern term which acknowledges that soldiers can become mentally scarred or deranged by the experiences of warfare. Very few people are natural killers. Soldiers who are trained to kill do not do so without conscience or independent thought; but sometimes things go wrong! Warfare sometimes creates 'monsters' who commit the most unspeakable atrocities, infinitely beyond any military or moral justification. Sometimes whole military units become indiscriminate executioners. I do not know why this occurs? Is it a breakdown of morale or discipline? Is it mass post-traumatic stress disorder? Or is it just wickedness?

After six years of modern, peaceful military service I returned to civilian life ... sort of. I became a Ministry of Defence police officer working with the defence community. My brief military service held me in good stead and over the next three decades and I was modestly successful in my policing career. Despite the close similarities of my two careers, I was surprised how difficult it was to adjust to being a civilian in uniform. As a police officer, good conduct and discipline remained paramount ... but it was different? I was not conditioned to obey orders, but I was compelled to uphold the Law; sometimes with the use of considerable force and often a daily experience!

Like all police officers I was trained to treat people with fairness, equality and sympathy. I learned the meaning of 'reasonableness' in its legal and ethical context ... a very important word when dealing with the lives and liberty of others. The Defence community that I served were, of course, supportive to law and order, but important military 'priorities' often clashed with the 'niceties' of civil policing. Nevertheless, the Defence community remained a part of 'greater society' and as such, were susceptible to the same human strengths and frailties that exist in the civilian world.

Thankfully, unlike their military colleagues, most police officers do not experience the wholesale slaughter of war; but they often meet injustice, violence, fear and tragedy at close hand. I inevitably experienced all of these things during my career ... it was part of everyday policing! As a result of over thirty years of dealing with crimes of violence and disorder, but also witnessing wonderful acts of courage and kindness, I have, I hope, developed a strong sense of both justice and toleration.

Some years ago I was on a touring holiday in France when I visited the site of what was once the remote and peaceful village of Oradour-sur-Glane. I learned that on a pleasant summer afternoon in 1944, a company of soldiers arrived at the village and within a few short hours and with military precision, they murdered nearly the entire civilian population; they then systematically destroyed every building using fire and explosives. Many decades had passed since the massacre, but the horrifying reality of Oradour's story left a lasting impression on me; my thoughts repeatedly returned not only to the victims, but to the soldiers ... how and why did they become 'monsters'? How could a whole company of well-disciplined young soldiers carry out the systematic mass-murder of defenceless civilians? Surely they were not all 'homicidal maniacs'?

Having been an inexperienced and untested soldier, who went on to become an old and very seasoned policeman, I felt the need to understand how and why this group of soldiers were driven to commit such a foul crime? I searched my own conscience, could I have been capable of such barbarity if I were placed in similar circumstances to those young men? I was chilled by my own uncertainties! Thus, I took it upon myself to find out more about the soldiers and their motivation to slaughter

642 innocent men, women and children.

Finally it is important that I emphasise that this book is not intended to be an academic account of the massacre at Oradour, nor of the criminal trials that followed. I know from long experience of establishing facts for legal purposes, that definitive evidence is always hard to come by. I have therefore relied upon the many professional publications about Oradour as my sources of information, and I accept that any mistakes in my interpretation of these works are solely my own.

*Roy Haines*

## CHAPTER 1

# Oradour Today

THE *NEW* TOWN OF ORADOUR-SUR-GLANE, BUILT shortly after the war, is unremarkable though not unpleasant in its modern architectural appearance. Just like most of the towns and villages of the Limosan region of central France, it is a busy, vibrant and peaceful community ... a good place to live, a good place to visit: modern homes, shops, hotels, schools and a new church. This bustling town stands a respectable few hundred metres from the old village, also once a happy, peaceful and prosperous place ... but its desolated grey ruins now exists solely to commemorate the victims of a foul crime and to warn mankind of its ability to become bestial when the peace breaks down.

The old village is accessed through a busy modern museum complex which provides the visitor with an abundance of information about the massacre: it strives to prepare us for what we are about to experience. As you move on, you pass through a short tunnel and enter the village ... and you are instantly taken back in time to the day of the tragedy. You are walking through the ruins of a peaceful community that abruptly ceased to exist on that fateful day, Saturday 10th June 1944.

The weathered grey ruin of the ancient Church of Saint Martin, is the most prominent structure: its bell tower overlooks the River Glane as it steers its way amidst the lush green Limosan countryside. The river gently flows by a water mill and under an old stone tram bridge, where the villagers used to gather for picnics and to sometimes fish for the plentiful trout during those peaceful summer days ... before the SS came. The rusting tramlines curve upwards from the bridge into the high street, Le Rue Emile Desourteaux. The Desourteaux family had been Oradour's leading dynasty for generations, providing many of its mayors, civil administrators, doctors and businessmen. Indeed, the mayor at the time of the massacre, Jean Desourteaux, was father to four sons who comprised of the village doctor, the town clerk, the village grocer and the garage workshop owner.

Today the village is tranquil and quiet; visitors are requested to respect the signs: 'Souviens-Toi Remember'. The horror that took place so many decades ago remains plainly evident today. As you enter the church you see the white marble altar and memorial plaques, which have been pierced and shattered by machine gun bullets. On the floor beneath the belfry is the curious sight of the melted bronze bell that once summoned the villagers to worship. There are no benches or prayer books; these were consumed by the flames that engulfed the church on that infamous day. Above the altar are three tall Norman windows that tell a story of death and survival. In the knave is the priest's grey wooden 'confessional' that miraculously survived the fire ... but it holds a terrible secret.

Outside the church the ruins of the houses, shops, cafes, garages, hotels and farm buildings have become weathered and faded; the decades of warm summer sunshine and mild winter rain have, to some extent anesthetised the destruction caused by the fires and explosives and bullets. Many of the homes bear memorial plaques listing the family members who fell victim to the SS that day; some display fading photographs of the murdered occupants.

Throughout the village the grass and shrubs and trees are neatly trimmed; the open spaces are tidy and bare. Ugly grey concrete pylons still carry the frayed electric cables that powered the little tram cars that once brought visitors from the nearby city of Limoges. During the war food had been scarce in the city, but the outlying villages had the benefit of the natural produce of the land; Oradour's hotels, cafes and shops had prospered as a result. Fading advertising boards and public notices identify some of the ruins: Hotel Milord, La Poste, Pharmacie, Boulangerie, L'ecole des Filles. Rusty iron gates and narrow alleyways provide access to the gardens and barns and stables that are now rubble and scorched timber. The barns and farm buildings remind us that this was a rural community which depended upon healthy livestock and fertile soil for its prosperity.

In the high street is a garage workshop; the back wall has little round holes blasted into the brickwork, at knee-height. Just inside the workshop is a rusting, 'sad-faced' old car, its dead headlamps gazing across the street towards the bakery. The cold rusty bakery ovens are surrounded by shattered glazed tiles and twisted bread racks. Someone has recently placed a little posy of crimson flowers at the oven door; a small token of remembrance for the infant victim of a particularly monstrous act of barbarity.

Just around the corner from the bakery is the village

green, Le Champs de Foire, with its little round communal well. Le Champs de Foire was the hub of the community; somewhere for the villagers to relax and chat, a gathering place for the monthly markets and the annual fun-fairs and civic ceremonies. Le Champs de Foire ... this is where the villagers were rounded-up by the SS before being herded off to their places of execution. Another rusting old car is parked at the edge of the green; it is believed by many to be that of the doctor, Jacque Desourteaux, who had returned to Oradour having completed his daily rounds ... only to be marched to his death with the rest of his fellow villagers.

The SS selected barns and storehouses throughout the village for their execution sites; the largest of which is known as the Laudy barn. It was in the Laudy barn that many of the menfolk were shot and their bodies burned. You can still see a small wooden door at the back of the barn that provided the escape and survival for a small band of young men. A pathway leads from the Laudy barn to an ancient cemetery where many generations of villagers are at rest. The more modern headstones bear the names of those of the community who survived the massacre, but for whom time has taken its natural toll ... it is here that they have chosen to finally rest near to their murdered loved-ones.

Overlooking the cemetery is a tall grey memorial column erected by the State to commemorate the victims. Beneath the column are two large rectangular glass-topped caskets which hold the dusty, grey ashes and bones of the four hundred and fifty or so women and children who perished in the church. It is difficult to ponder and stare at these stark remains. It is perhaps insensitive to display them so publically, but it is nevertheless, a potent and unforgettable symbol of the massacre.

In the burnt and ruined houses and out-buildings throughout the village there is a multitude of domestic artefacts that remind us of the villagers' lives before the killings. In the living rooms and kitchens are ornate hearths and stoves with rusty cooking pots; on the window sills are sewing machines ... lots of sewing machines. In most of the homes are the remnants of electrical wiring; thus reminding us that although rural and remote in its location, Oradour was a modern community with many of the household devices that we are accustomed to today. There is an abundance of rusting bicycles and motor cars throughout the village, providing yet more evidence of the liveliness and prosperity of the community.

The tram station and sidings are situated near the top of the high street. Sadly, it was the local tramway system that inadvertently brought many additional victims to the village on the day of the tragedy: visitors from the city, eager to food-shop or to dine in the cafés and hotels, or simply to spend a few pleasant hours fishing on the River Glane for supper. Overlooking the tram station is the ruin of the Post Office; a once grand and ornate building. Across the street is the town hall and residence of Mayor Jean Desourteaux and his family.

Prior to being appointed as mayor, Jean had been the village doctor; he had handed over his medical practice to his son Jacques some years previously. Near to the town hall is the linen-ware shop of the prosperous Dupic family; across the street are the remains of their large and imposing house. Monsieur Dupic kept a fine wine cellar and an abundant kitchen ... something that did not go unnoticed by the SS. Further down the high street are the bleak, grey ruins of the shops, cafés, hotels, garages, the blacksmith's forge, the wine store and the homes of over six hundred murdered villagers.

At the lower end of the village and along the high street, are the ruins of four separate school buildings. Oradour had provided education for infants and older girls and boys; and there was an additional school for the refugee children whose families had escaped from the Alsace and Lorraine regions, the first areas of France to be invaded by the Germans at the beginning of the war. From one of many such refugee families, came little Roger Godfrin, aged seven years ... Roger was one of only two small children who survived the massacre.

The Alsatian refugee families had fled northern France in hope of avoiding 'Germanisation' or worse, by Hitler's occupying authorities. Roger's family had been welcomed by the villagers and were living in a hotel in the high street. Another refugee family living in Oradour were the Pinedes', who were Jews. Ominously, young André Pinede was the other small child who survived the massacre. The refugees were especially aware of Nazis intolerance. Refugee parents constantly advised their children to run and hide if the Germans ever came to Oradour. Sadly the local village children were not so accustomed to the brutal capabilities of the Nazis, and on the day of the massacre they had compliantly followed orders given to them by the soldiers. As a result, they had all perished in the church, alongside their teachers and the village womenfolk.

So there the 'martyred' village of Oradour-sur-Glane remains ... a tragic ruin, a bleak, empty and decaying memorial in the heart of the beautiful Limosan countryside. Despite great efforts by the French authorities to maintain its crumbling structures, the village is gradually weathering and fading. Many household and personal artefacts have been moved to the security of the museum or have simply disappeared; probably taken by souvenir hunters over the decades since the massacre. Many of the walls and roofs and floors of the homes and buildings have collapsed to rubble. The bullet holes and the fire damage have eroded over the years, making the horror just a little less evident. There is littering in some places; a rather irreverent but perhaps inevitable consequence of admitting many thousands of public visitors to the site each year. Some areas of the village look almost tranquil, particularly in the grassed and cultivated areas around Le Champs de Foire and opposite the church.

The decision of General De Gaulle in 1945 to preserve the village, in order that the horrors that took place there should not be forgotten is clearly vindicated. But as the story of the massacre slips from living memory, the village of Oradour has become a more educational place. The museum complex provides vivid displays and artefacts that keep the spirit of De Gaulle's intentions alive. The ruins of Oradour-sur-Glane are the only place in Europe where people can directly witness the stark reality of war and what it sometimes brings to an ordinary peaceful community. So why and how did this tragedy happen? What were the political, military and criminal aspects of history that led to the massacre at Oradour ... and who was responsible?

CHAPTER 2

# France and Germany – Historic Enemies

TO UNDERSTAND THE OPPOSING CULTURES OF THE people of Oradour-sur-Glane and the SS soldiers who murdered them in the summer of 1944, we must go back to the previous generations of France and Germany. For many years the peoples of northern France and southern Germany endured frequent phases of open warfare followed by periods of uneasy peace. Both countries made claim to the sovereignty of the border regions of the Alsace and Lorraine. By 1870 Chancellor Otto Von Bismarck, had united all of the individual Germanic states to form the new nation of Germany ... but the Alsace and Lorraine regions remained beyond his grasp!

Predominant amongst the German people were the Prussians who were wealthy, elitist, militaristic and technically advanced. Germany was rapidly gaining massive industrial and military strength, and Bismarck's eye was firmly focused on the Alsace and Lorraine. The shift in military power was greatly favouring Germany, and the French, fearing Germany's growing power, pre-emptively declared war. This monumental mistake resulted in defeat for the French and the loss of the Alsace and Lorraine regions, which were duly subjugated by the victorious Germans. The conquered people of these regions were no longer deemed to be French, but German citizens. It is ominous that during this brief but bloody war, the German army committed many atrocities against captured French soldiers and the civilian population of Northern France. This was a clear indication of the German army's attitude and practices that were destined to be grossly repeated during future conflicts.

By contrast, hundreds of miles to the south of the German border, the peaceful and prosperous village of Oradour-sur-Glane remained unaffected by the defeat. But Oradour's Mayor, Emile Desourteaux, a predecessor of Jean Desourteaux, was very aware of the ever-increasing aggression and military strength of Germany. The people of Oradour shared the fears and festering resentment of their northern countrymen ... would German strength continue to grow? Would the Germans one day burst through their borders and occupy the remainder of their beloved France?

Triumphant Germany lauded over France's defeat. Prince Wilhelm, Germany's young and psychologically unstable heir to the throne, had pretensions of building a German Empire to rival that of his British grandmother, Queen Victoria, whose colonies and subjugates straddled the world. Despite being born with a withered and useless left arm and acquiring an almost uncontrollable temper, Wilhelm had been groomed since childhood to become a professional soldier ... and he was also poised to inherit dictatorial powers over his people.

When he finally came to the empirical throne in 1888, Kaiser Wilhelm began a modern arms-race with both France and Great Britain. Nevertheless, for two further decades, a fragile and uncertain peace prevailed between Germany and France ... but it became clear that war would be inevitable. Much diplomatic and political appeasement took place by the world's leading statesmen to avert a European war. Indeed, Wilhelm's cousin, King Edward VII of Great Britain was able, to some extent, use his personal charm and family ties as a calming influence upon the excitable Kaiser. But Wilhelm and Germany's powerful Prussian military elite remained determined to pursue their imperialistic desires.

When King Edward died in 1910 hopes of European peace began to fade. The defeat of France remained Wilhelm's first priority and he secretly sought an opportunity to strike! In the summer of 1914 he used an obscure crisis in the Balkans as an excuse to execute his well-prepared invasion plans. The German army trampled over their peaceful neighbour Belgium, committing acts of atrocity against the civilian population as they crossed into Northern France. But the Great War, 'the war to end all wars', ended four years later with Germany's humiliating defeat and Wilhelm's abdication. The Alsace and Lorraine regions were duly returned to France. The war-weary citizens of these much disputed regions were once again deemed to be French. Far to the south, the people of Oradour-sur-Glane continued with their peaceful existence, reassured that the threat of the Germans ever reaching their beautiful village was now very much diminished.

But the devastation and carnage of the World's first global conflict did nothing to stifle the empirical desires of a great number of the German people. Indeed it was the Treaty of Versailles, which imposed debilitating war reparations upon Germany and the return of the Alsace and Lorraine to France, which inevitably ignited the fires of Nazism. In 1933 Adolf Hitler, another psychologically unbalanced leader, fanatically drove the Nazis to power and became the dictator of Germany. The *Fuhrer's* imperialistic ambitions exceeded even those of Wilhelm. His power-lust was fuelled by his deep resentment of Germany's defeat in the Great War and his fear of Communism, which he viewed as a Jewish-led plot for world domination. In 1939 having subjugated several defenceless smaller nations, Hitler invaded Poland. Both France and Great Britain were compelled by treaty to defend the Poles and World War Two began.

By the summer of 1940, for the third time within seventy years, the full thrust of the German army spilled into Northern France. Once again the peoples of the Alsace and Lorraine became subjugated Germans; but this time the expectation was that Germany would go much further and occupy all of 'Mother' France. Hitler's Blitzkrieg, 'lightning-war' knew no bounds, his military power and ambition seemingly insatiable ... and unbeatable!

Further south in the Limosan region, Mayor Jean Desourteaux and the villagers of Oradour-sur-Glane, pragmatically prepared themselves for occupation by the Germans. Petrol was strictly rationed and cars were laid-up in garages and lock-ups; the annual fairs at Le Champs de Foire were cancelled. Some young men had left the village to fight the Germans ... some had not returned! The remaining young men of the village braced themselves to the possibility of deportation to Germany as industrial slave workers. But mercifully the invasion did not reach Oradour ... no conquering Germans arrived? Ominously, Oradour was geographically located within the new unoccupied-zone called 'Vichy' France, under the puppet-government of the elderly Marshall Philippe Petain.

The people of Vichy France were not deemed to be as troublesome as those living in the northern French regions adjoining the German border, so the creation of the Vichy government was a convenient arrangement for Hitler. He did not wish to use his soldiers as occupational 'policemen'. He was poised to invade Russia and needed his fighting troops for his ever-expanding empire in Eastern Europe. By collaborating with the Nazis, Philippe Petain, a French hero in the Great War, believed himself to be the saviour of his people ... but he nevertheless bowed to the directions of his Nazi puppet-master.

Indeed, Petain actively supported Hitler in his endeavours to annihilate Communism, which had thrived in both France and Germany during the previous decades ... and like Hitler, Petain was an anti-Semite. He promptly took the opportunity to utilise his political militia, 'La Milice', to round up thousands of his Communists and Jewish countrymen and arranged their deportation to Germany as slave workers ... Or, in the case of the Jews, sent them directly to the Nazi death camps.

But eventually, world-wide events intervened. In 1941, Japan's attack on Pearl Harbour triggered America's belated entry to the war, forcing Hitler to robustly defend his European empire. He now faced two major battle-fronts: the Russians to the East and the Anglo-Americans, imminently poised to invade the southern and western coasts of France. Hitler also faced another 'front' from within his empire ... the Resistance movements.

Despite Petain's subservience to the Nazis, he could

not prevent Hitler from finally occupying Vichy France. Ominously, Vichy France was the temporary home of thousands of refugees who had fled the path of the Nazis at the beginning of the war. But remarkably, life in Oradour still carried on almost as normal for both the villagers and their refugee guests. The occupying Germans were rarely seen by the villagers, but the Alsatian Godfrin family and the Jewish Pinede family were now not quite so certain of their safety in this peaceful and remote village. The children of both families had settled comfortably into their new homes and schools, but their parents had never let them forget that the Germans might suddenly turn their attentions to Oradour, "If the Germans come, run and hide"! Without doubt, it was this constant alertness that would go on to save the lives of the three Pinede children and little Roger Godfrin!

## Chapter 3

# Refugees

WHEN ARTHUR AND GEORGETTE GODFRIN AND their five young children arrived at Oradour in the summer of 1940, they must have been very relieved to be far from their home town of Charly in northern France. The occupying Germans now deemed Charly and every other town and city in the Alsace and Lorraine to be part of the Third Reich! The refugee families knew that their homes and previous way of life were lost; at least for the foreseeable future.

The refugees had arrived at Oradour with nothing but the few possessions they were carrying, but they were the lucky ones! Thousands more refugees, men, women and children, fleeing their homelands and seeking refuge elsewhere, had been mercilessly machine-gunned from the air by the Luftwaffe. When these desperate refugee families began to arrive in Oradour, Mayor Jean Desourteaux generously ensured that they were provided with homes in the heart of the community and a special school for the refugee children was set up at the lower end of the village.

Little Roger Godfrin, then aged just four years and his four brothers and sisters took little time to integrate with the local village children; they began to discover the joys of their new life, playing games with their new friends in Le Champs de Foire and along the river banks

## Chapter 3: Refugees

near the watermill and the tram bridge. Roger had little understanding of the terrifying events that had brought him to his new home, but his father Arthur, knew only too well that their security in this lovely village remained subject to the whims of the Nazis who might turn their attentions to Oradour and at any time.

The Godfrins' and the other refugee families had lived under the Nazi threat throughout the previous decade and were well accustomed to the hatred, fear and intolerance that had infected every part of their community in the Alsace and Lorraine. They knew of the brutality exercised by the Nazis against anyone deemed to be *undesirable*. The horrors of the detention camps for enemies of the State were well known to the vulnerable northern French population; although safe and newly housed in distant Oradour, Arthur Godfrin took every opportunity to instruct his children, "If the Germans come, run and hide"!

The Jewish refugee family, Robert and Carmen Pinede and their three children arrived at Oradour in 1943. Robert, who was a veteran soldier of the Great War, also brought along his elderly mother, Gabrielle. They had fled their home city of Bayonne near the Spanish border for very different reasons. They had been forced by the occupying Germans to register as Jews; their family business had been confiscated and they had no means of income. They had no illusions as to what their fate would have been if they had remained in their home city ... remote and distant Oradour must have seemed a much safer place.

Jaqueline Pinede, the oldest child, was an olive skinned pretty young woman, likewise her younger sister

Francine; their brother André, was afflicted with Down's syndrome, but was otherwise a healthy and happy young boy. The family were allocated rooms in the Hotel Avril in the high street and the Pinede sisters soon proved to be a popular attraction for the young men of the village; particularly during the community dancing events. But as Jews, Robert and Carmen were very aware of the consequences if the Germans ever came to Oradour. They had already experienced the reality of the Nazi Race Laws in their home city of Bayonne. They knew that throughout Germany and some of the French regions, Jews were forbidden to use public places such as parks, theatres and swimming pools. They were forbidden from employment by the State, which meant many Jewish civil servants and teachers lost their means of income; Jewish doctors could not practice except on other Jews. Even distinguished Jewish lawyers, university professors, scientists and internationally famous musicians were forbidden from practicing their professions. The Race laws stripped Jews of their nationality, which meant that they had few human rights and no protection from the State. The Nazi newspapers, radio stations and cinemas spewed out Joseph Goebel's anti-Semitic propaganda. Little Jewish children were bullied and beaten by their Aryan school friends. Jews were attacked in the streets whilst the police looked on and did nothing; any Aryan suspected of sympathising with the Jews risked criminal charges and detention by the Gestapo.

The Nazis were beginning to round-up Jews and incarcerate them in concentration camps for the slightest of excuses; with the advent of the war, all Jews were deemed to be enemies of the state. Robert and Carmen

Pinede realised that it was only a matter of time before the Nazis fully enforced their Race Laws throughout France. They had already fled for their lives from Bayonne and they knew that they would receive little mercy if the Germans ever came to Oradour! Robert Pinede ensured that Jaqueline, Francine and André were given the same instructions that Arthur Godfrin had given to his children: "If the Germans come, run and hide"!

Mayor Jean Desourteaux, made sure that the refugees were afforded not only homes and education, but he also found employment for many of the adults within the community. This gave the refugees the dignity of financial independence and a means to provide food and comforts for their families. The rationing of food to the civilian population of France was getting ever-tighter, particularly in major cities like nearby Limoges; but rural Oradour had the advantage of its natural abundance of crops and livestock. The villagers and the refugees did not starve. Indeed, in the hotels, cafes, bakeries and shops, business was bolstered by visitors from the city, where food rationing was more strictly administered. Compared to Limoges, everyday life in Oradour was good ... ample rations and no Germans!

The villagers of Oradour were a traditional Roman Catholic community; nevertheless, they extended their spiritual support to the refugees, many of whom were of the Protestant and Jewish faiths. Despite the ever-present threat posed by the Germans, the villagers made life for the refugees as normal as possible. As the months passed, the refugees gradually settled into their new homes and way of life. Indeed their spirits were further lifted in the spring of 1944 when unofficial news began to secretively circulate throughout France: the tide of the war had turned! The Allies were on the offensive!

The combined American, British, Canadian and exiled French armed forces were of such strength that it was obvious that the Allied Invasion of France was imminent! Despite the absence of any Resistance activity in Oradour, rumours indicated that the *Maquis* in other Limosan towns and villages, were well-armed and very keen to fight alongside the Allies. Was it possible that Oradour would soon be liberated? Could it be that the Germans would never come to the village? Was it possible that the refugees would be able to return to their homes in the Alsace and Lorraine? Could the Pinede family return to their home city of Bayonne near to the Spanish border? Hopes were cautiously rising!

CHAPTER 4

# The Soldiers

THE SS (SCHUTZSTAFFEL), WERE ORIGINALLY A very small group of Nazi party members whose sole purpose was to provide personal protection for Adolf Hitler; each took an oath to dedicate their lives in pursuance of this sacred duty. Their slightly-built and weak-chinned leader, Heinrich Himmler, selected only the most 'Aryan' of these fanatical volunteers. In fact the newly formed SS rank and file were the complete opposite to their leader in appearance! Each soldier had to be a perfect specimen of manhood; they were tall, fair skinned and physically strong. Any SS volunteer with the slightest physical defect was rejected! Their ancestry was rigorously investigated and any candidates suspected of having 'Jewish blood' were immediately excluded, no matter how far back in their family history this proved to be.

Prior to the war, Hitler and Himmler knew that the SS, in contrast to the *regular* German army, could be totally depended upon to carry-out their Nazi party doctrine without question. The SS were 'political' soldiers who were trained and conditioned to be totally ruthless; and they were prepared to die for their Fuhrer. Back in 1934 Hitler, despite his dictatorial powers, still had many political opponents within his party whom he considered a threat to his leadership; so he simply ordered the SS to murder them! During the infamous 'Night of the Long Knives' Heinrich Himmler and his exclusive band of SS assassins, shot in cold-blood, hundreds of people known or suspected of being opposed to Hitler.

In 1939 at the outbreak of war with France and Great Britain, the SS had grown from a few hundred volunteers to nearly 800,000 members! The political gerrymandering of Himmler had incorporated within the SS's control all of Germany's police forces, its intelligence services, its political secret police (Gestapo) and the guards at the concentration and death camps. Additionally, Himmler took the opportunity to create his own private army which he named the Waffen-Schutzstaffel, the Fighting SS!

Waffen SS soldiers were always at the forefront of battles and fought fanatically and courageously, but inevitably casualties were extremely high! As the war progressed, recklessly brave young SS men were dying by the thousands on the vast battlefields of Russia! By now, replacement SS recruits of the Aryan standard were becoming much more difficult to come by. Eventually Himmler was forced to compromise and began filling the gaps in the SS ranks with teen-aged boys conscripted directly from the Hitler Youth movement. Although the Hitler Youth guaranteed recruits of Aryan lineage and ideals, they were not in any way battle-wise and subsequently died in their droves! Many of the SS guards from the concentration camps and death camps were subsequently transferred to Waffen SS divisions throughout Europe. Eventually, replacement SS troops began to be transferred-in from the *regular* German army or were conscripted directly from the civilian community, including young men from the subjugated

## Chapter 4: The Soldiers

French regions of the Alsace and Lorraine. Some of the Waffen SS divisions were not even German, but had been made-up of volunteers and conscripts from the defeated nations of Holland and Norway. Nevertheless, all of the SS fighting divisions remained under the command of a hard-core of seasoned and experienced German officers and NCOs, who remained unwaveringly committed to Nazi ideals! They were tough, fanatical and ruthless ... and totally loyal to Hitler!

By the time that the Germans had occupied the Alsace and Lorraine regions of Northern France in 1940, the Nazis had acquired nearly two decades of experience in 'institutionalised' brutality. The general population of the Alsace and Lorraine were historically divided into those of Germanic descent, who generally accepted the German invaders as liberators, and those of French allegiance, who did not. Thousands of families, like the Godfrins' chose to flee to the safety of the towns and villages of Vichy France, including Oradour-sur-Glane; but most Alsatians remained in their homes and resigned their fate to the Germans.

A minority, but significant number of the population of the Alsace were emphatically pro-Nazi. Georges René Boos was a strapping seventeen year old youth who had no allegiance to his French Alsatian countrymen, and couldn't wait to become one of the Fuhrer's elite soldiers. As soon as he was able, Boos volunteered to join the SS; a significant number of young French Alsatian men did the same! Thousands of other, less-enthusiastic, Alsatian men did not volunteer; but they were nevertheless conscripted into the regular German army. Georges René Boos not only volunteered to join the SS, but he was as fanatical as any member of Hitler's new breed of Aryan soldiers; he excelled as a recruit and was quickly identified for early promotion. The casualty-rate of fighting soldiers in the SS was horrendous and replacements were in constant demand. By the age of just 20 years, Georges René Boos had achieved the rank of Scharführer (Sergeant) in the Der Fuhrer Regiment of the elite Waffen SS 2nd Panzer Division ... 'Das Reich'!

In 1941, Hitler had sent the SS Das Reich division to Russia as part of his invading army; the infamous Operation Barbarossa. The Das Reich division fought fanatically against the unprepared Red Army and achieved many military successes, but their achievements were not without penalty. When they arrived in Russia, Das Reich were a full fighting division of 19,000 soldiers, by 1943 barely half of the battle-weary troops remained. Following in Das Reich's footsteps into Russia came the SS Einsatzgruppen 'execution' battalions. The Einsatzgruppen's purpose was the elimination of partisans, commissars (communist political officials), Jews and anybody else deemed to be an enemy of Germany. Although Das Reich were an SS fighting division, they, and many regular German army units, assisted the Einsatzgruppen in some of the worst atrocities against the Russian civilian population. The Nazi Holocaust had begun in earnest but was still yet to meet its peak of monstrosity!

By the spring of 1944, having retreated from Russia, the Das Reich division were 'resting' in Southern France. The commanding officer, Gruppenführer (General) Heinz Lammerding, did not delay in rebuilding his division ready for the next battle to come: the long awaited

'Second Front', the Allied Invasion of Western Europe! As the commander of an elite SS fighting division, General Lammerding faced the dilemma of lack of suitable recruits. The Das Reich division now comprised of the depleted and battle-weary hard-core of fanatical SS soldiers, newly bolstered by French Alsatian conscripts of extremely limited fighting ability ... and of dubious loyalty.

Long gone were the glory-days when the Waffen SS could demand only the fittest and Aryan of the youth pool. Lammerding's new recruits were a hotchpotch of inexperienced and physically inferior troops with little or no inclination to fight the Allies. When the opportunity arose, many of the Alsatian conscripts deserted the SS and joined the Resistance. Many went on to fight gallantly against their former German masters.

Heinz Lammerding had only recently been appointed as commander of Das Reich and was only 38 years of age; although a long-standing Nazi party member, he was not held in the highest esteem by some of his Waffen SS contemporaries. In civilian life, Lammerding was a professional engineer and had earned a reputation as a competent administrator; but his more battle-experienced SS contemporaries considered that he lacked the combat experience and the competence necessary for high military command. Nevertheless, Lammerding was a close friend of Heinrich Himmler and as such his willingness to invoke the most extreme and cruel measures against his enemies, particularly the Resistance movement, was not in doubt!

As Das Reich rested in southern France, Lammerding's administrative and organisation skills had greatly assisted in the rebuilding of the division to its full strength of

19,000 troops. The division was also re-equipped with new tanks and artillery in preparation for the battle to come. Although there remained many shortfalls of weapons, transport and equipment, Das Reich still retained a sufficient hard-core of officers, NCOs and soldiers of fighting experience to maintain its status as an 'elite' panzer division. Das Reich was therefore considered to be battle-ready and vital to the German defence of occupied France. But in reality, Lammerding's officers and NCOs were deeply concerned that their French Alsatian recruits could not be relied upon to fight the Allies, unless the harshest of disciplinary measures were instilled. Lammerding therefore instructed his officers to be zealous and utterly ruthless in applying such measures.

One of Lammerding's keenest young officers was Untersturmführer (Second Lieutenant) Heinz Barth. As a boy Heinz Barth had been a member of the Hitler Youth and at the outbreak of war he joined the regular German Army; he then volunteered to transfer to the SS. Groomed in Nazi doctrine since childhood, Barth showed that he could be depended upon to carry out the most extreme and unsavoury commands of his superiors; and he exhibited a natural zeal for brutality! In 1942 in Czechoslovakia, Barth had been ordered to command firing-squads at several villages that had been selected for reprisals following the assassination of SS Obergruppenführer, (General) Reinhard Heydrich.

Known as the Butcher of Prague, it was Heydrich who had been the mastermind behind the Nazi death camps and gas chambers, and he was also the creator of the infamous SS Einsatzgruppen execution battalions. It was even mooted that Heydrich was destined to become

Hitler's heir to the Reich. Winston Churchill and the Czech Government in exile realised that Heydrich was too dangerous to remain alive and sent a team of agents to carry out his assassination in Czechoslovakia. The operation proved to be successful and Heydrich was fatally injured by a hand grenade thrown by his assassin as he travelled to his command post in the centre of Prague.

Nazi revenge was inevitable and swift and Hitler personally ordered mass reprisals against the Czech population. The Czech agents were quickly tracked-down, but chose to fight to the death rather than surrender to the Germans. But the Nazi reprisals continued. Second Lieutenant Heinz Barth and hundreds of other German officers carried out their odious reprisal orders with compassionless efficiency; many thousands of innocent Czech men, women and children were summarily executed. It is ominous that the atrocities and destruction that occurred in the Czech village of Lidice on the 10th June 1942, where the entire male population were murdered, took place exactly two years prior to the massacre at Oradour-sur-Glane. Heinz Barth had the dubious honour of being actively involved in both of these infamous Nazi atrocities.

After his service in Czechoslovakia, Heinz Barth was drafted to the Waffen SS in Russia where he continued to add to his growing 'curriculum vitae' of brutality. By June 1944 Barth, still holding the lowly rank of second lieutenant, and now serving with the Das Reich division, was in charge of a platoon of soldiers, resting near the city of Toulouse in southern France. One of Barth's platoon NCOs was the fanatical French Alsatian volunteer, Sergeant Georges René Boos.

Boos was detested by his fellow Alsatian soldiers; his pro-Nazi and bullying manner were completely alien to the young French conscripts. Boos was equally detested by the German soldiers in his platoon. Nevertheless Barth, Boos and the other battle-weary SS veterans of the Russian campaign must have been greatly relieved to be far away from the fighting in Russia and enjoying the relative comfort and peace of southern France ... albeit that the Allied Invasion was expected at any moment!

General Lammerding, well aware that his 'hotchpotch' of recruits lacked battle experience, knew that Adolf Hitler was relying on his elite SS panzer division to counter-attack the Allies on the landing beaches ... wherever they proved to be? Lammerding also knew that if the Allies could not be driven back into the sea, Germany would lose the war! In the relative peace of southern France there was little opportunity for the recruits to become 'mentally' conditioned and toughened for the battle to come; but the pragmatic Lammerding took every opportunity to use his troops to assist the Gestapo and Phillipe Petain's Milice in apprehending and executing civilians suspected of Resistance activities.

Pending the Invasion, even in Vichy France the Resistance were becoming far more troublesome to the occupying Germans; the execution of civilian hostages as reprisal measures were therefore becoming more and more commonplace. The experienced SS Das Reich veterans were well acquainted with the brutal reprisal operations that the division had carried out in Russia, and they were determined to use these same methods to eliminate Resistance activities in France! The situation also provided the opportunity for the SS veterans to acquaint their French Alsatian recruits with some of the less-savoury tasks that was to be expected of them! During the spring and summer months of 1944, SS Das Reich would go on to participated in the execution of hundreds of civilians in reprisal operations throughout southern and central France, the most infamous of which was soon to take place at the remote and peaceful village of Oradour-sur-Glane!

## Chapter 5

# Resistance

THROUGHOUT FRANCE, LEADERSHIP AND discipline within local Resistance groups varied considerably. Many of the fighters and their families had suffered terribly during the occupation and there was a burning desire for revenge against the Germans and any French men or women deemed to be collaborators. The temptation by local Resistance leaders to carry out counter-reprisals against the Germans sometimes proved overbearing. Both Churchill and De Gaulle recognised that the provocation of the occupying Germans prior to the Invasion, might significantly compromise the Resistance's capability to carry out their primary and vital role of Sabotage!

The Allies foresaw that the Resistance would be key to delaying the German forces from reaching the landing beaches. A successful sabotage operation could tip the balance in favour of the Allies; thousands of lives could be saved! Resistance leaders were therefore ordered *not* to carry out unauthorised attacks against the Germans; but these orders were often ignored. Inevitably, the consequence of Resistance counter-reprisals against German troops meant even greater reprisals against the civilian population; and significantly ... increased Gestapo operations to eliminate Resistance units that were a vital component of the Invasion plan!

## Chapter 5: Resistance

By the spring of 1944 the 50,000 or so Resistance members throughout France, were at their peak of fighting potential and keen to assist the Allies! Churchill's SOE (Special Operations Executive) agents and SAS soldiers had been parachuted throughout France and had achieved considerable success in uniting the fragmented multitude of local Resistance groups; albeit with considerable difficulty! As a result of the efforts by the SOE and the SAS, leadership, weapons training and radio communication systems within the Resistance movement were greatly improved. Throughout France firearms, explosives and other essential military equipment had been secretly distributed to Resistance groups. The Resistance fighters were enthusiastically poised to sabotage the roads and railway networks that the Germans were expected to use to convey their troops, tanks and artillery, as they sped towards the Allied landing beaches.

The Resistance were also poised to destroy telephone networks in order to disrupt and confuse the Germans when the Invasion came. Sabotage of transport and communications would prove vitally important during the earliest stages of the Invasion. Delaying or preventing the German troops reaching the landing beaches would significantly assist the Allied Forces in the establishment of their 'beachheads' and would aid their advance to vital military targets further inland. Another important role of the Resistance was to assist the SOE agents in gathering intelligence such as the location and strength of German military divisions ... including General Lammerding's SS Das Reich!

But not all was harmonious amongst the Resistance fighters. Local Resistance groups were generally divided

## Chapter 5: Resistance

by their political ideals. The so-called Free French Resistance allegiances lay with General de Gaulle's government in exile in England; but the Communist Resistance, who were particularly active in the Limosan region, were inspired by the doctrines of Stalinist Russia. Each of these ideologically opposed Resistance groups aspired to achieving political power in France when liberation came! Inevitably, a bitter rivalry existed between many of the Resistance units. The military objectives of the SOE and the SAS in co-ordinating the vast array of Resistance groups therefore proved to be extremely difficult; nevertheless they all shared one vital, common objective ... the defeat of the Germans!

The Allied commanders and the Resistance leaders were well aware that the Limosan region encompassed many of the roads and railway networks that were vital to the movement of German troops from southern France to the northern coastline. This presented the Resistance with the opportunity to sabotage the routes that the Das Reich division were expected to travel along in order to intercept the Allied landings. The cities, towns and villages of the Limosan were soon to be overwhelmed by tens of thousands of German soldiers frantically trying to reach the Normandy beaches; but first they would have to do battle with vengeful, highly motivated Resistance fighters, who sought to sabotage and delay their every movement. Determination, anger, fear and revenge would arise amongst the fighters of both sides; the toxic flames of reprisals and counter-reprisals were increasing by the day!

In the peaceful and remote village of Oradour-sur-Glane there was no Resistance activity. The general

## Chapter 5: Resistance

feeling amongst the villagers and the refugees was that they had been fortunate enough to have been ignored by the Germans throughout the whole four years of the occupation, so why should they provoke the situation, particularly as it was likely that France would soon be liberated by the Allies? But this attitude was not shared by all French communities, particularly those who had been subjected to German brutality and had subsequently formed active local Resistance groups.

One such centre of Resistance activity was the village of 'Oradour-sur-Vayres'. As well as sharing a name, both villages were situated in the remote countryside of the Limosan. The two villages were also strikingly similar in size and appearance, and significantly, only 30 miles apart. Both villages were also situated at an equal distance of twenty miles from the city of Limoges. Strangers to the Limosan region could be forgiven for mistaking the two communities!

## Chapter 6

# Invasion

IN THE EARLY HOURS OF TUESDAY 6TH JUNE 1944, thousands of American and British airborne troops began to land at the extremities of the 60 mile long Normandy coastline. Just a few hours later, an armada of some 5,000 Allied ships and landing craft began to spill wave after wave of soldiers, tanks and artillery onto the beaches. The long awaited Allied Invasion, Operation Overlord, had begun! The future of the free-world completely depended on the success of the Allies to not only secure a foothold on the beaches that day, but to quickly punch through the German's defences before they had the opportunity to counter-attack ... if Overlord failed, Europe might never be freed from Nazi tyranny!

Hitler was dependent upon his elite Panzer divisions to destroy the Allied forces before they could consolidate their beachheads. But the Panzer divisions were sparsely dispersed at holding locations along the whole of the 2,000 miles of French coastline, awaiting Hitler's personal orders to strike back at the Allies. Should the German counter-attack succeed, then the Allies would be driven back into the sea. Overlord would fail! But on that pivotal day, Hitler remained uncertain whether the Normandy beaches were the true Invasion location or merely a diversionary attack? He had been duped by the Allied counter-intelligence services into believing that the

## Chapter 6: Invasion

*real* Invasion would take place much further north near Calais. Confused and indecisive, Hitler refused to allow his generals to send their Panzer divisions to Normandy. This was a monumental mistake by the Fuhrer and by the time that he realised that Normandy was the *true* Invasion location, the Allies were already beginning to advance inland.

Nevertheless, the military situation remained pivotal; there was still a chance that the Panzer divisions could stall the Allied advance and then drive them back into the sea. Hitler was now dependent on the Panzers to speedily proceed from their dispersed holding positions to the Normandy beaches. But now was also the time and opportunity for the Resistance to do the job that they had trained for: sabotaging the roads and railways, destroying the telephone networks, delaying the Panzer divisions from reaching Normandy! Hundreds of eager local Resistance groups carried out their sabotage attacks with reckless courage; miles of telephone cables were cut ... confusion reigned!

The work of the Resistance proved to be particularly disruptive to the Panzer divisions stationed in southern France. Just outside of Toulouse, 450 miles south of the Normandy beaches, General Lammerding's SS Das Reich division, was totally dependent on the roads and railways to convey his soldiers and tanks to the Allied beachheads; but first they would have to run the gauntlet of the Resistance! In order to quell the Resistance's enthusiasm, Lammerding did not hesitate to order yet more reprisals against the civilian population of the towns and villages in his path. Tragically, and contrary to Churchill and de Gaulle's orders, some local Resistance leaders began to order counter-reprisals against the Germans ... a horrifying tit-for-tat sequence of atrocities began to emerge!

For over two years a small garrison of *regular* German army soldiers had been based in the town of Tulle, some eighty miles to the south of Oradour-sur-Glane. The German garrison's relationship with the local French population had been relatively passive throughout the occupation, but the situation had rapidly deteriorated following the Invasion. On Wednesday the 7th June, a local Resistance group, well-armed and hell-bent on revenge, overwhelmed and slaughtered many of the German soldiers in the garrison. This flagrant breach of discipline by the Resistance had tragic consequences for the civilian population of the town. The very next day Tulle was retaken by General Lammerding's SS troops as they frantically advanced northwards towards the Normandy beaches.

Upon discovering the mutilated bodies of their regular army comrades, the SS soldiers rounded-up the men and older boys of the town and began to execute them by hanging them from the street lamps and balconies along the high street. Ninety nine men and boys were murdered this way, and a further one hundred and fifty were deported to Germany as slave-workers or were sent directly to the concentration camps ... few ever returned! General Lammerding's French Alsatian recruits were rapidly becoming accustomed to the extreme 'anti-terrorist' measures required of them by their SS masters!

Das Reich carried out dozens of reprisal actions against the civilian population as they frantically progressed towards Normandy; but the Resistance groups remained equally determined to delay them. On Thursday the 8th June, many of General Lammerding's infantry troops were travelling by train towards the railway bridge which spanned the River Vienne near the town of St Junien; just eight miles from Oradour-sur-Glane. To Lammerding's frustration, the bridge had been severely damaged by explosives planted by the local Resistance group, and several German soldiers had been shot as they attempted to cross the wreckage of the bridge on foot.

Although the 19,000 strong Das Reich division had a massive military superiority, the SS soldiers were only too aware of the consequences should they fall into the hands of the Resistance? The frustrations of delay and fear of capture by the Resistance, only added to the SS commander's determination to use reprisals to discourage Resistance attacks. But Petain's Milice, until now considered to be loyal to the Germans, had been spooked by the activities of the local Resistance at St Junien. Following the attack on the rail bridge, the mayor of St Junien spoke to the local head of the Milice and informed him that there were many hundreds of armed Resistance fighters in the area awaiting orders to carry out further attacks. This veiled warning by the mayor, certainly quelled the Milice's determination to assist the SS in finding the saboteurs! The Milice knew that the Vichy Government's days were numbered and they would soon have to answer for their collaboration with the Germans!

Things came to a head in the isolated Limosan countryside, when SS Sturmbannführer (Major) Helmet Kämpfe, foolishly travelling alone by car, was ambushed and captured by the local Resistance. Kämpfe, was the holder of the Iron Cross and other high military honours, and was a popular officer within the Das Reich division. General Lammerding, who had set up his temporary headquarters in Limoges, promptly ordered a massive search operation throughout the local towns and villages in order to find the missing officer.

Coincidentally, another SS officer, Obersturmführer (Lieutenant) Karl Gerlach, was also captured by the Resistance and taken to an unidentified village to the east of St Junien. Despite being stripped of his clothing, brutalised and then witnessing the execution of his SS driver, Gerlach miraculously managed to escape and then make his way through twenty miles of countryside to the safety of General Lammerding's headquarters in Limoges. Gerlach reported that he had seen a road sign somewhere near to the place that he was captured, which read 'Oradour-sur-Glane'. Subsequently, an immediate decision was made to search the village in the hope of finding Major Kämpfe. Ominously, the similarly named village of Oradour-sur-Vayres, an active centre of Resistance operations, was totally ignored during the Germans searches for the missing officer.

CHAPTER 7

# Search Plans

THOUSANDS OF DAS REICH SOLDIERS WERE spread out around the Limosan region including the city of Limoges. Sturmbannführer (Major) Adolf Diekmann's infantry battalion was particularly active in the area of Saint Junien, and he was therefore the obvious choice to lead the search operation at Oradour-sur-Glane. It remains unclear whether General Lammerding specifically approved or selected Diekmann for this task; but he was known to be one of the General's most experienced and dependable officers.

Diekmann chose a company of some 150 soldiers, led by Hauptsturmführer (Captain) Otto Khan, to carry out the search at Oradour. Both Diekmann and Khan were veterans of the Russian campaign and were typical products of the SS academy: Diekmann tall, blond and athletic, Khan tough and stocky. Both officers were committed to Nazi ideals ... and both totally ruthless! Diekmann was also a friend of the captured officer, Helmet Kämpfe; his motivation for achieving success, both personally and professionally was not in doubt. Diekmann would carry out his 'search' operation zealously, and with little regard for the lives of the men, women and children of Oradour-sur-Glane!

Just prior to the Allied Invasion, as sabotage operations and attacks on German troops had begun to increase, Hitler had directed his senior commanders to issue 'reprisal' orders that were intended to give German military officers a degree of 'legal' confidence to carry out 'anti-terrorist' counter-measures against the Resistance. Field Marshall Hugo Sperrle was the Commander in Chief of the German Forces in France, and was therefore responsible for drafting such orders. The pompous Sperrle, who was a crony of Reich Marshall Herman Goering, was a Luftwaffe officer, but in reality, he had few airborne resources at his command; the RAF and US Airforce had destroyed most of his aircraft during the build-up to D Day. Nevertheless, Sperrle did not hold back on his language when reiterating the Fuhrer's command regarding reprisals; his written 'anti-terrorist' orders were explicit and uncompromising:

'Units in southern France to proceed with extreme severity and without any leniency'.

'The forces of the resistance are to be crushed by fast and all-out effort'.

'The most rigorous measures are to be taken'.

'Ruthlessness and rigour at this critical time are indispensable'.

'If troops are attacked there is to be an immediate return of fire ... if innocent people are hit, this is regrettable but entirely the fault of the terrorist'.

'All of the civilians in the locality, regardless of rank and person, are to be taken into custody'.

'Houses from which shots have been fired are to be burned down on the spot'.

'A slack and indecisive troop commander deserves to be severely punished, because he endangers the lives of the troops under his command, and produces a lack of respect for the German forces'.

'Measures that are regarded subsequently as too severe, cannot in view of the present situation, provide reason for punishment'.

This final paragraph, clearly implies that no punishment will be taken against officers whose actions are retrospectively regarded as too severe! Major Adolf Diekmann and his officers were therefore confident that they had the 'legality' to impose the most brutal measures, when carrying out the search operation at Oradour-sur-Glane. Diekmann knew that with men like second Lieutenant Heinz Barth of the infamous Czech massacres and the fanatical French Alsatian volunteer, Sergeant Georges René Boos leading his troops, every order would be carried out with compassionless efficiency. However, Captain Otto Khan, knew that his conscripted French Alsatian recruits would require a considerable amount of enforced discipline, in order to carry out their 'search' duties. Khan therefore instructed his officers and NCOs to lead their soldiers by example. Adolf Diekmann, Otto Khan, Heinz Barth and Georges René Boos would soon be let off the leash; the fate of Oradour-sur-Glane was soon to fall into the hands of fanatical SS bullies who would stop at nothing to find their missing comrade.

In reality, following his capture two days previously, Major Kämpfe had been taken to the regional Resistance leader, Georges Guingouin, who ordered that he should be summarily executed ... which was immediately carried out by his revenge-hungry resistance fighters. It cannot be ascertained whether Major Kämpfe was executed before or after the massacre at Oradour; years later, Georges Guingouin stated that he had ordered the execution of

Kämpfe after he had heard of the massacre at Oradour. But Guingouin, who after the war became the mayor of Limoges, disclosed few details of when or how Major Kämpfe had been executed. Years later Kämpfe's remains were eventually discovered and were reburied at the town of Berneuil in central France.

On the afternoon of Friday 9th June 1944, Major Diekmann instructed Captain Khan and Second Lieutenant Barth to meet him at the Hotel De La Gare, which overlooked the railway bridge in St Junien that had been sabotaged by the Resistance the previous day. It was within the walls of the hotel that Diekmann and his officers then set about their preparations to 'search' Oradour-sur-Glane. Diekmann, using the experience he had gained alongside the SS Einsatzgruppen execution battalions in Russia, settled upon a well-practiced pincer operation: The village would be surrounded by SS troops forming a secure perimeter; meanwhile other SS soldiers would enter the village and round-up the population on the village green. A systematic search of every building and dwelling would then be carried out. To aid their search operations, the SS had learned that it was advantageous to select hostages in order to extort information. They had also learned that the destruction of people's homes was also an effective means of gaining the cooperation of the local populous.

Diekmann reasoned that if Major Kämpfe was indeed held captive at Oradour, his search operation would prove to be successful. During the previous days, Otto Khan and his company had carried out a similar 'search' operation at the village of Frayssinet le Gelat, where they had executed 15 hostages, including an 80 year old woman. They had

## Chapter 7: Search Plans

then looted and burned many of the villagers' homes. This atrocity may well have been the reason why Diekmann had specifically selected Khan's company for the search operation at Oradour.

General Lammerding's searches for Major Kämpfe did not just rest at Oradour-sur-Glane; hundreds more SS and regular German army soldiers were scanning the city of Limoges and the towns and villages of the Limosan in the hope of finding the missing officer. Tragically, an important British SOE agent, Violette Szabó, who had been parachuted into France in order to gain vital intelligence during the D Day operation, had been inadvertently discovered and captured during Lammerding's expansive search operations.

Disguised as a civilian worker, Violette had used her charm, beauty and fighting courage to achieve her intelligence gathering objectives. Her work was invaluable to the success of the Allies during the early days of the Invasion, but her successes were cut-short by Lammerding's searches for Major Kämpfe. After a valiant gun fight against an overwhelming number of German soldiers, Violette was captured, then interrogated and tortured by the Gestapo. She was later taken to the Ravensbruck concentration camp in Germany, where she was murdered together with two other captured female agents. Their bodies were incinerated in the camp ovens.

Had Violette *not* been captured by Lammerding's troops, she would have continued to carry out her vital work of keeping the local Resistance units focused on their primary role of sabotaging Nazi road, rail and communications networks and, most importantly, keeping the Allied command informed of German troop movements. Following the war this courageous young woman was posthumously awarded the George Cross by the King, and a motion picture 'Carve Her Name with Pride' was made in her honour.

CHAPTER 8

# Saturday 10th June 1944

ON SATURDAY 10TH JUNE 1944, ORADOUR-SUR-Glane awoke to an uncharacteristically dull and wet dawn. The villagers breakfasted and went about their daily tasks in the same manner as villagers had done for centuries; cows needed to be milked and crops needed to be tended. The Mayor, Jean Desourteaux and his youngest son Etienne, his administrative secretary, took the opportunity to clear their desks in preparation for the following week's busy civic responsibilities; there was also the important tobacco distribution to be overseen that day. Tobacco was subject to wartime rationing, and the weekly issue, mostly to the men of the village, required precise administration and control in order to ensure fairness and to reduce black-market abuse.

Doctor Jacques Desourteaux, who had taken over the village medical practice when his father became mayor, made sure that there was enough petrol in the tank of his Citroen 'Berline' to carry out his rounds of the out-lying villages and farmsteads that day. He hoped to complete his rounds and return to the village by early afternoon, in order to ensure that a visiting health team had completed their scheduled medical examinations of the village's school children.

Another of the mayor's sons, grocer Paul Desourteaux, prepared his wares for the morning shoppers. On

Saturday mornings customer numbers were boosted by weekend visitors from Limoges, hungry to subsidise their meagre city rations. The tram cars would soon be arriving at the station next to the Post Office, disembarking eager customers to the high street shops and cafés.

Hubert Desourteaux, yet another son of the mayor, left his home and walked the short distance to his garage workshop in the high street. Although most of the villagers' cars were temporarily stored in barns and gardens because of petrol rationing, there was always plenty of engineering work to be done. No new cars could be acquired, because virtually all industrial manufacture in France had been taken over by the German 'war-machine'. Private cars still in use, agricultural vehicles and machinery required skilled maintenance and repair; Hubert's business was therefore always busy, even during the weekends. The men of the Desourteaux family were indeed the very hub of Oradour's peaceful and prosperous community.

One of the earliest risers that morning was 44 year old baker Maurice Compain whose bakery and shop overlooked the village green on Le Champs de Foire. The bakery ovens needed to be fired, dough and pastry mixed, trays, cooking pots and utensils laid-out in order to ensure his Saturday morning loaves, baguettes, buns and rolls were warm, fresh and baked to perfection. Maurice knew that his friend and business rival, Léopold Boucholle, whose Boulangerie was just around the corner in the high street, would also be a hive of activity! But their friendly rivalry inevitably benefitted everyone. On a busy Saturday in the middle of summer, the demand upon both bakeries would be continuous throughout

## Chapter 8: Saturday 10th June 1944

the day. The ovens would be in constant use, producing batch after batch of fresh bread for the villagers and their city visitors. It would be the very last time that Léopold Boucholle's ovens served their peaceful purpose ... in just a few short hours they were destined to become the scene of unimaginable barbarity.

The village priest, Jean-Baptiste Chapelle, took the opportunity to prepare his church for the following day's Sunday worship. Oradour was a traditional Roman Catholic community and a high turnout was always expected from the congregation. Jean-Baptiste was much respected for his devotion to his flock; the 71 year old priest thought nothing of walking many miles throughout the local countryside each day to tend to the spiritual needs of his more frail or sickly parishioners. Spiritual wellbeing had become crucial in these desperate times; families craved the mental strength to suffer the loss of a son at war, or a refugee's loss of home and way of life. Jean-Baptiste was always there, always strong.

Many of the refugees spoke in a heavily accented northern French dialect and were of the Protestant or Jewish faiths; but Jean-Baptiste ensured that their spiritual needs were met according to his versatile and generous Christian principles. This was particularly important to the Alsatian refugees whose language and culture were sometimes uncharitably ridiculed by a small number of the villagers; the old wooden 'confessional' in the church was in much demand during these troubled times. Jean-Baptise had become a little frail in recent years, and he had taken on the services of a housekeeper; and he was sometimes assisted in his duties by Jacques Lorich, a refugee priest from the Moselle, a sub-region of

## Chapter 8: Saturday 10th June 1944

the Lorraine in northern France; yet another community that had endured decades of Franco-German aggression.

In wartime-France, children attended school on Saturday mornings. This particular day was expected to be especially demanding for the village's school teachers as the children were to be given examinations by a visiting medical team. It was anticipated that some of the younger pupils might become distressed by the procedures, so the teachers were keen to ensure that fun and games were also included to belay any anxieties. Few such anxieties would affect seven year old refugee Roger Godfrin. This plucky young lad had already impressed many of the villagers by his adventurous and mischievous nature ... these very qualities in one so young, were to prove vital to his survival that very day.

Jean-Marcel Darthout and his young wife Angéle, lived with his mother in a small house near to the village churchyard. Jean-Marcel was a keen member of the village football team, but as no fixture was to take place on that particular Saturday, he awoke in a more leisurely way, enjoying his breakfast before busying himself with work around the house. Jean-Marcel, like many of the young men of Oradour, was well aware that the Nazis sometimes abducted fit and able young men and deported them as slave workers to the German war factories. But he was also comforted by the knowledge that the Allies would soon be advancing through France, forcing the Germans to retreat to their homeland. He reasoned that his chances of being taken into slave-labour were reducing by the day.

Another young villager, Paul Doutre, was not so assured. As a 21 year old single man, he viewed himself as particularly vulnerable to abduction by the Nazis. He reasoned that although the Germans had not yet come to Oradour, things could change rapidly. He anticipated that following the Allied Invasion, the Germans were far more likely to abduct slave-workers for vital war manufacture. It was Paul Doutre's fear of the Nazi's slave-labour policies that probably saved his life that day.

Armand Senon was a tough and spirited young man; like Jean-Marcel Darthout he was a member of the village football team. However, Armand had had the misfortune to have broken his leg in a recent match and was forced to wear a plaster cast and to use a wooden crutch to move around. Armand was mostly confined to his house and garden which faced onto Le Champs de Foire, but as each day passed, he began to exercise his legs around the village centre. As fate was to be, Armand's garden with its array of mature bushes, apple trees and undergrowth proved to be crucial in saving his life later that day!

The Beaubreuil brothers, Joseph and Maurice, resided in the family home which adjoined their father's carpentry workshop on the lower outskirts of the village, alongside the River Glane. At the outbreak of the war, Maurice had served as a soldier in the French army, but following the French surrender, he had been held as a prisoner of war by the invading Germans which proved to be a brief, but extremely unpleasant confinement for the young man! Upon release and his subsequent return to Oradour, Maurice remained deeply distrustful of the Germans and vowed never to become their prisoner again. On that wet Saturday morning the two brothers were visiting their aunt, Jeanne Mercier, at her house in the high street, just opposite to the church. Some repairs were needed to the stonework of Jeanne's house and she had employed a local stone mason, Mathieu Borie, to carry out the work during that morning. Mathieu's masonry skills would prove crucial to his survival and that of four others later that day!

The Hébras family resided in the high street midway between Le Champs de Foire and the tram station. The head of the household, Jean Hébras, was a retired tramway electrician, but he still did some part-time work as a farm labourer and had left the village earlier that morning to work in the outlying countryside. Jean's wife, Marie and son Robert, an 18 year old mechanic, remained at home together with sisters, 22 year old Georgette and little Denise who was aged 9 years. Young Robert's work place was in a garage in Limoges, nearly an hour's journey by tram, but he took comfort in the fact that he was not required to work on that wet and cloudy Saturday morning. During the previous two days, Robert's boss at the garage had noticed that since the Invasion, the German soldiers in Limoges had become far more intolerant towards the civilian population; he considered that the younger men might prove to be particularly vulnerable to the soldiers' aggression, and so he had advised Robert to stay at home until things became a little more settled!

In the relative safety of his remote and peaceful village, Robert optimistically anticipated that the morning rain would soon clear and the mid-summer sun would burst through, promising a pleasant and restful weekend. Robert loved his village and could not envision anywhere else more suited to spend his days. He adored his parents and sisters and was well liked and respected by his fellow villagers. Just like Armand Senon and Jean-Marcel Darthout, Robert was a keen footballer. For

## Chapter 8: Saturday 10th June 1944

a healthy young man residing in a beautiful, prosperous community, life could not have been more promising. Robert's spirits were further boosted by the knowledge that the Germans would soon be expelled from his beloved France; his ambition was to become a good mechanic and perhaps own his own garage one day? Life's opportunities seemed really good for young Robert Hébras on that fateful morning.

Next to the Hébras' house was the Hotel Avril, the temporary home of the Jewish refugee Pinede family. Robert and Carmen Pinede, together with their daughters 18 year old Jacqueline and her 16 year old sister Francine, busied themselves with household chores. Nine year old André was left to play around the apartment. As a Down's syndrome child, André did not attend the refugee school and remained at home with his parents. André's two pretty older sisters, who had proven to be such a great success with the young men of the village, looked forward to getting out and about as the anticipated sunshine warmed through the high street and Le Champs de Foire.

Next door, the Alsatian refugee housewife, Georgette Godfrin, washed and dressed her children in readiness for school. Marie-Jeanne aged 13 years, Pierette aged 11 years and little Roger aged 7 years, would soon join the village's school children for their lessons and the scheduled medical examinations. Roger's younger brother and sister, Claude and Josette remained at home. As they left for school, Georgette reminded her children for the final time, "If the Germans come, run and hide!"

Marguerite Rouffanche resided with her husband Simon, her son Jean and her daughter Andrée at a small farm on the outskirts of Oradour. Marguerite's oldest

## Chapter 8: Saturday 10th June 1944

daughter, Amelie Peroux and her husband and baby son Guy, lived nearby. Marguerite was a typical example of sturdy, rural French womanhood; being born and raised in a farming family, her days were always occupied cooking, washing, cleaning and carrying out a multitude of domestic tasks. Saturdays were no different to any other day to a farming family in Oradour; livestock and crops to be tended to, washing to be hung, meals to be prepared. Some blessed rest might come the following morning after the family's Sunday worship at the church. Marguerite had regularly attended the Church of Saint Martin since childhood; fate was soon to decide that 47 year old grandmother, Marguerite Rouffanche, would be the only person to survive of the four hundred and fifty women and children herded into the church, then systematically asphyxiated, shot and incinerated by the SS, later that day!

As the morning progressed, the clouds dispersed, the sun brightened and the people of Oradour-sur-Glane, happily went about their peaceful and prosperous business. The trams began to arrive from Limoges filling the cafés and shops with eager customers. School lessons began, farmers tended their livestock, bakers and pattissiérs tended their loaves and pastries. Spirits were high; the Allies were advancing! Liberation and freedom from Nazi tyranny must come soon! Who could possibly have perceived that their future would be anything other than peace, prosperity and happiness? Tragically, the morning of Saturday 10th June 1944, was to be the very last few hours of life that the ancient village would ever know.

It was during that cloudy and wet morning, just

## Chapter 8: Saturday 10th June 1944

eight miles away that Major Adolf Diekmann formed up his military convoy of trucks and half-track troop carriers near to the railway station at St Junien. The SS officers, NCOs and their hotchpotch of German and French Alsatian soldiers boarded their vehicles and then proceeded to the small village of St Victurnien. Diekmann then halted the convoy and the troops were given a final briefing by their platoon commanders. Heinz Barth emphasised to his NCOs and men, "today you will see blood flow". The SS recruits were left in no doubt of the extreme nature of their mission that day! St Victurnien was just a few miles from the tram bridge at the entrance to Oradour-sur-Glane. After their brief pause, the SS convoy continued their fateful journey ... within minutes the people of Oradour-sur-Glane would hear the unfamiliar sound of heavy vehicles approaching their village.

Photographs and Illustrations

2. Oradour-sur-Glane in better times

3. Rue Emile Desourteaux today

Photographs and Illustrations

*4. The boucherie kitchen in the high street*

*5. A 'sad-faced' old car gazes across the High Street*

Photographs and Illustrations

6. *Hubert Desourteaux's garage workshop - Bullet holes at knee-height*

7. *Most of the villager's cars were stored in lock-ups for the duration of the war*

*8. The excitable Kaiser Wilhelm II*

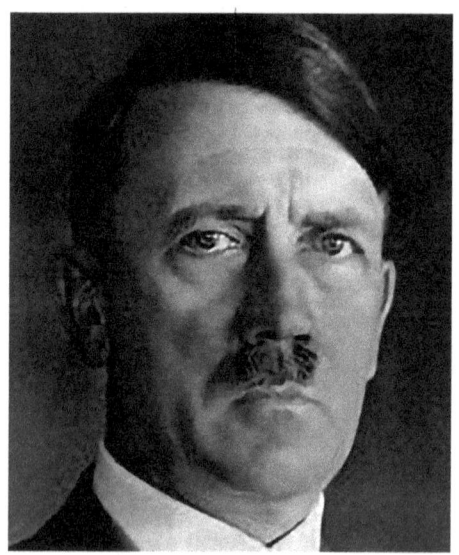

*9. Adolf Hitler - Another psychologically unbalanced leader*

Photographs and Illustrations

10. Vichy President Phillippe Petain and his Nazi puppet-master

11. 'Dealing with the opposition' A newspaper cartoon c.1934

12.

*Heinrich Himmler - SS Reichführer*

13.

*Reinhard Heydrich - Mastermind of the Holocaust*

Photographs and Illustrations

14. June 6th 1944 Normandy - Operation 'Overlord' the Allied Invasion

15. Petain's 'La Milice' round-up their fellow countrymen

*16. Tulle - An SS officer's sketch of the hangings*

*17.*

*Captured SS officer - Sturmbannführer Helmut Kämpfe*

Photographs and Illustrations

*18. The Church of Saint Martin before the massacre*

*19. The 'other' Oradour - A recent image of Oradour-sur-Vayres*

Photographs and Illustrations

20.

*The local Resistance Leader Georges Guingouin, who ordered the execution of Sturmbannführer Helmut Kämpfe*

21.

*Violette Szabó, George Cross - The courageous SOE agent*

Photographs and Illustrations

22.

*The pompous Field Marshal Hugo Sperrle - Author of the 'reprisal orders'*

23.

*Gruppenführer Heinz Lammerding - Das Reich division commander*

24.

The 'monstrous' Sturmbannführer Adolf Diekmann who planned and executed the massacre

25. Experienced killers: Untersturmführer Heinz Barth (left) and Hauptsturmführer Otto Khan (centre)

# Photographs and Illustrations

26. *The Hotel De La Gare in Saint Junien, where Diekmann planned the massacre*

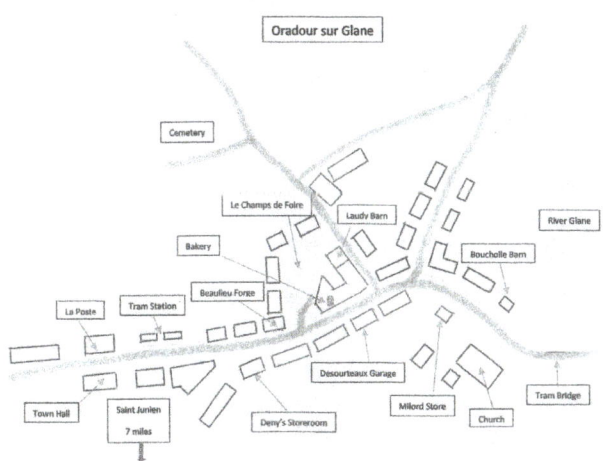

27. *Map of Oradour-sur-Glane*

CHAPTER 9

# The SS Arrive

IT WAS JUST AFTER LUNCHTIME THAT GARAGE owner, Hubert Desourteaux's trained mechanic's 'ear' perceived the faint rumbling of heavy traffic approaching the village ... very heavy traffic! Hubert instinctively realised that the vehicles were military. It was much too early for the American or British forces to have reached this far south of the Normandy beaches, so it could only be the Germans! Hubert had served as a soldier at the beginning of the war, and like Maurice Beaubreuil, he had been briefly held as a prisoner of war by the Germans. He too, was determined never to become a captive again, and he immediately took refuge near to his workshop courtyard.

At 1.45pm Major Diekmann's convoy paused briefly at the tram bridge at the entrance to Oradour; several trucks then diverted from the convoy and made their way across the open countryside surrounding the village. Soldiers were dropped off at predetermined locations ensuring that the village was totally sealed-off. The trap was set! SS troops then began to round-up the men, women and children residing in the outlying houses and farms near to the village. Marguerite Rouffanche and her family had just finished their lunch when the soldiers arrived at their home. She and her family were ordered to quickly get aboard an SS truck where they were informed that they

## Chapter 9: The SS Arrive

would be transported to the village centre for identity checks. Though very frightened, Marguerite reassured her daughters and granddaughter that all would be well, the identity checks would soon be over and they would then be permitted to return to the farm.

Meanwhile, the leading half-track vehicles broke away from the convoy and sped across the tram bridge, travelling along the full length of the Rue Emile Desourteaux to the top end of the village. Hubert Desourteaux, caught site of the half-tracks, each full of German soldiers, as they thundered past his garage workshop. The vehicles then turned around near to the Post Office and then returned back down the high street to the tram bridge. Many fears passed through Hubert's mind; would he be suspected of being a resistance fighter? Would he be abducted as a slave-worker? Would he be taken as a hostage or worse? Hubert immediately made up his mind to remain hidden. His cautiousness would prove to be crucial to his survival that day; but not without tragic consequences!

Having reported to Diekmann that the village did not present any hostile capability, the soldiers in the half-tracks re-formed with the main convoy at the tram bridge. Diekmann then ordered the convoy to move forward to Le Champs de Foire in the village centre. SS troops then swiftly alighted from their vehicles and began to fan-out through the streets and houses, aggressively ordering the people to go immediately to the village green for identity checks. Mayor Jean Desourteaux made his way to Le Champs de Foire, where he identified himself to Major Diekmann. The SS commander explained that he intended to carry out full identity checks of the villagers and would also carry out a search of all premises for arms and explosives. It is unclear whether Diekmann stated to the mayor that he was also looking for the missing SS officer, Helmut Kämpfe. But Diekmann did make it clear to the mayor that he expected total compliance from the villagers, otherwise the consequences would be very severe.

Diekmann then instructed the mayor to select twenty hostages to be held to account if there was any lack of cooperation by the villagers. The mayor bravely protested and suggested that he personally, together with his four sons, would more than suffice if hostages were to be selected. Diekmann seemed to accept this compromise.

Meanwhile, in the pleasant early-afternoon sunshine, the people of Oradour-sur-Glane, together with their Saturday visitors, began to nervously assemble on the village green at Le Champs de Foire. But some of the people of Oradour were determined not to come to the attention of the SS. Ex-prisoner of war Hubert Desourteaux remained concealed near to his workshop. Paul Doutre, in fear of abduction as a slave-worker, hid in his garden shed. The other ex-prisoner of war, Maurice Beaubreuil and his brother Joseph, determined never to be taken into the custody of the Germans, decided to conceal themselves in the home of their aunt near to the church. Injured footballer, Armand Senon, realising that his chances of escape were highly unlikely, hid in his bedroom where he could see the SS soldiers rounding up everyone in Le Champs de Foire.

The Jewish refugees, Robert and Carmen Pinede although terrified, instructed their children, Jaqueline, Francine and André to hide under the stairway of the Hotel Avril; but Robert and his wife, having no means of

## Chapter 9: The SS Arrive

concealment for themselves, resignedly joined the rest of the villagers at Le Champs de Foire. Arthur and Georgette Godfrin, the Alsatian refugees, also had no choice but to obediently make their way to the village centre. They prayed that their children, Jeanne-Marie, Pierette and little Roger, who were still at the refugee school at the lower end of the village, would 'run and hide' from the Germans, as they had so frequently been told.

The SS soldiers quickly forced their way into every building and ensured that the occupants were marched off to Le Champs de Foire. They made no exceptions, any villager deemed too slow to obey, received the end of a rifle butt or some similar form of violent encouragement. As the soldiers entered the four school buildings, many of the children became distressed, however, the teachers somehow managed to maintain order and ushered the youngsters along the high street to the village centre. But little Roger Godfrin, only seven years of age, kept a cool head. He clearly remembered his parents' oft-repeated instructions, "If the Germans come, run and hide". Roger quickly found his sisters and begged them to join him, but they were too distressed and followed their school friends and teachers to Le Champs de Foire. Unnoticed, Roger calmly walked out of the refugee school building and made his way to the undergrowth by the River Glane, where he temporarily concealed himself. But Roger's ordeal had only just begun.

Within a few minutes, with the exception of those in hiding and a few elderly and bed-ridden people, over six hundred villagers, refugees and their Saturday visitors, had assembled at Le Champs de Foire. Most of the people, although very nervous, seated themselves on the grass

## Chapter 9: The SS Arrive

in small groups. The young mechanic, Robert Hébras, sat with a group of his friends from the football team and made comforting small-talk about forthcoming match fixtures. As they did so, the young men saw the mayor speaking to the German commander, and they also nervously noted that they had been surrounded by SS troops wielding rifles and machineguns! The baker, Maurice Compain spoke to one of the SS guards and requested to attend to his ovens, which he feared might cause a fire, but he was assured by the soldier that this would be attended to.

At some point, a French-speaking soldier addressed the crowd and stated that all villagers were to declare whether they held any firearms. One man said that he owned a hunting gun but was in possession of a permit; which seemed to be acceptable to the SS commander. As the minutes passed things settled down, but suddenly the soldiers began to bark orders at the men and older boys to move away from their families and friends. They were then instructed to form a separate group at the edge of the green.

Shortly after this, the soldiers ordered the women and children to stand up. They were then all marched under escort to the church, where they were instructed to sit on the benches situated either side of the aisle. The inside of the little church was soon brimming with four hundred and fifty or so very nervous women and distressed children. Marguerite Rouffanche, together with her daughters and grandson, seated themselves on the benches near to the marble altar, facing the three elongated Norman windows above the aisle. Their SS guards stood at the entrances to the church, ensuring that no one escaped. Minutes passed and the women and children gradually settled down, albeit that they were all deeply worried about their menfolk and the older boys.

Back at Le Champs de Foire, the SS then ordered the hundred and ninety or so men and boys to separate into five smaller groups. Each group was then marched-off to different locations throughout the village. Little Roger Godfrin, still hiding by the riverside, heard the women and children being marched into the church; he also heard a group of men and boys being marched to Monsieur Boucholle's barn nearby. The barking orders of the Germans unnerved Roger, so he decided to move further along the river bank.

In the high street, Hubert Desourteaux, still hidden near to his garage yard, heard a group of men being forced into his workshop only metres away. Hubert could clearly hear the SS shouting orders at the men and boys as they nervously crammed into the small and confined building. He could also distantly hear other groups of men being escorted into the Beaulieu Forge at the entrance to the village green, and into the Hotel Milord storeroom near to the church.

Hiding in his bedroom overlooking Le Champs de Foire, the incapacitated but spirited Armand Senon, was determined not to be apprehended; he clung on to his wooden crutch in readiness to use it as a weapon against the soldiers. Just around the corner, hidden under the stairwell of the Hotel Avril, the three Jewish Pinede children, held their nerve. They could hear a group of men and boys being marched along the high street, and then being crammed into Monsieur Denis's wine store just opposite to their hotel. Young Paul Doutre, fearing abduction as a slave worker, remained concealed in his garden shed. Each one of these villagers continued to hold their nerve and remained hidden. It would prove to be a terrifying but lifesaving ordeal.

The young mechanic Robert Hébras, was in a group of about sixty men and boys who had been marched the short distance from Le Champs de Foire to the Laudy barn, in the cemetery road. The barn was a large structure, but it was crammed with carts and other bulky agricultural equipment. The Germans had difficulty in forcing all of the men into the barn, so they ordered them to remove the contents to make space. Once the men and boys had cleared the barn sufficiently, they were instructed to stand inside and await further instructions.

As the minutes passed, Robert noticed that his fellow footballer, Jean-Marcel Darthout was also in his group. Crucially, also in the group were the stonemason, Mathieu Borie, together with Yvon Roby, a young postal worker, Clement Broussaudier a deliveryman and Henri Poutaraud a garage worker. Although very alarmed, the young men still assumed that the purpose of their incarceration within the barn was for identity checks, and to allow the Germans to carry out searches of the other buildings. But tensions rapidly escalated when the soldiers set up two heavy machine-guns just outside of the barn, but facing inwards and directly towards the men and boys. Real fear began to set in, but the soldiers then seemed to settle down again. A long and silent pause of activity by the soldiers transpired, and several of the men thought that they heard music being played from somewhere within the village? Perhaps one of the soldiers had discovered a radio?

## Chapter 9: The SS Arrive

The SS had carried-out exactly the same procedures at the other predetermined locations throughout the village: the Boucholle barn near the tram bridge, the Milord Hotel storehouse near to the church, Hubert Desourteaux's garage workshop in the high street, the Beaulieu Forge next to Le Champs de Foire, Monsieur Denis's wine store in the high street and the Church of Saint Martin, crammed full with 450 terrified women and children! Minutes passed, the soldiers did nothing. But they remained alert and intense behind their heavy machine guns!

## Chapter 10

# Carnage

IT WAS MID-AFTERNOON IN THE REMOTE AND beautiful Limosan village of Oradour-sur-Glane. The summer sun hovered brightly over this peaceful community which had existed for a thousand years. An enforced silence had descended upon the empty streets and houses. The four hundred and fifty or so womenfolk and children sat on the benches of the ancient church, guarded by armed SS soldiers. In barns and storehouses throughout the village, the menfolk and older boys stood in terror, facing SS soldiers who were wielding rifles and heavy machine guns.

The SS commander, Adolf Diekmann and his deputies Otto Khan and Heinz Barth, were experienced killers. What they were about to do, they had done previously in Russia and Czechoslovakia. Their French Alsatian 'bully-boy' henchman, Sergeant Georges René Boos was straining at the leash; he could be trusted to carry out his orders with perverse zeal. The experienced German SS veterans knew exactly what was expected of them, but for their inexperienced French recruits, most of whom were teenagers, this was to be their initiation to SS mass-murder operations. They were each well aware that their own lives were subject to forfeit, should they fail to carry out their orders.

Major Diekmann's 'search' operation was going

completely to plan. The village was under his complete control, the villagers were restrained and compliant, and his soldiers were at their predetermined positions. He now decided it was time for the eerie silence to be broken. A barked military order was immediately followed by a loud burst of gunshots which resounded though the village. This was the signal for the killings to begin!

Standing in the Laudy barn young Robert Hébras, with a group of some sixty men and boys, heard the signal shots in the distance. Facing them at the entrance, the SS men laying prone behind their heavy machine-guns suddenly opened fire spraying bullets left and right ... left and right! Within the confines of the barn the noise of the machine guns was as deafening as it was deadly! All around him, Robert could see and hear the men and boys as they screeched in pain and terror as their shattered bodies fell to the floor of the barn. Robert instinctively dropped to the floor with the others. The machine guns continued to fire and Robert sensed the bullets as they blasted through the air just centimetres above his head.

After the long initial burst, the machineguns were suddenly silent. Stupefied and shocked, but alive, Robert immediately began to focus his thoughts! The stench and smoke from the bullets filled the air. Daylight beamed through the entrance, but it was comparatively dark within the barn. Robert remained motionless in the hope that the soldiers would not notice him! He guessed correctly that there would be others in his group who also remained alive.

A long and silent pause transpired, but gradually Robert began to hear the pitiful groans and pathetic cries of those terribly injured men and boys still clinging to life.

## Chapter 10: Carnage

The SS, it seemed, had patiently waited for this moment in order to identify those still living. Robert heard soldiers moving amongst the fallen men and boys, occasionally dispatching a pistol or rifle shot. There then followed another long and silent pause. Robert could hear, but could not understand the SS soldier's subdued conversation, but he prayed that the SS were now convinced that all of the men and boys were dead.

A few minutes passed and Robert cautiously began to think that the soldiers might go away. But his optimism evaporated when the soldiers began to collect straw bales and wood and began to throw them over the prostrate bodies on the barn floor. Robert then realised that the SS intended to finish-off any survivors by burning the barn! His fears were confirmed when a soldier set light to the straw. Smoke and fire immediately began to spread through the building. Robert heard the soldiers closing the doors from the outside and the barn was briefly consumed in darkness, but then flames and thick acrid smoke quickly began to fill the air.

Robert realised that he must quickly find a means of escape or perish in the fire. Getting to his feet proved to be more difficult than he expected. He had been wounded in the arm during the initial burst of machine gun fire and his movement was constricted by the bodies of several other men who had fallen upon him. But a desperate desire to survive motivated Robert to get to his feet. He then desperately began to seek a means of escape from the barn! Robert knew that the SS soldiers were guarding the barn doors from the outside and poised to finish-off any escapees. What could he do to escape the rapidly spreading smoke and flames?

As fate would have it, Robert was not the only survivor within the burning barn. His fellow footballing friend Jean-Marcel Darthout was also alive, but had been wounded in both legs and had great difficulty in being able to stand! But Jean-Marcel's survival instinct was strong and he forced himself to his feet! Robert and Jean-Marcel could hear the pathetic pleas and groans of other men and boys who were desperately clinging on to life. But the inferno was engulfing them at a merciless pace. The blinding smoke and flames prevented any efforts by Robert and Jean-Marcel to save the wounded and the dying, but miraculously, out of the melee appeared four other men! They were Yvon Roby, Clement Broussaudier, Henri Poutaraud and crucially, the stonemason Mathieu Borie. Each of the six young men were suffering from the inhalation of the acrid smoke as they made frantic searches for a means of escape. They considered forcing open the barn doors, but they knew this would be met by a hail of machinegun fire from the SS guards outside, so they instinctively felt their way along the inside wall towards the back of the building.

Unknown to the SS guards, there was a small wooden door at the back of the barn. The six men in desperation, managed to force open the door and found themselves in a small walled enclosure. Their brief hope of escape was dashed when they realised that they were surrounded on all sides by solid stone walls, and they could find no means of escape from the rapidly advancing smoke and flames. Having no choice, they re-entered the burning barn to search for another escape route! Mathieu Borie, the stonemason, frantically examined the heavy brickwork at the back of the barn and found what he hoped to be the weakest point of the construction. Using only his hands, Mathieu began to loosen the bricks and mortar and eventually managed to make a hole large enough for the men to crawl through. They then found themselves in a narrow passage-way which led them to some brick-built rabbit hutches. Beyond the hutches they could see the open green space of Le Champs de Foire!

Although the rabbit hutches were very cramped, the men managed to hide themselves within, but the flames were relentlessly progressing towards them. From their concealed position they could see the pathway which led from Le Champs de Foire to the cemetery, but they could also see and hear the SS soldiers patrolling nearby. Jean-Marcel's leg wounds were now causing him extreme pain and he begged the others to leave him and to escape across the green to the cemetery pathway, which was just twenty yards away. The young men knew that if they could get to the cemetery it would be feasible to escape into the woodland surrounding the village, but they were reluctant to leave the badly injured Jean-Marcel behind.

The flames were now beginning to engulf the rabbit hutches and it would only be a matter of time before they were burned alive. In desperation, Henri Poutaraud made a dash across the open green and managed to get to the pathway, but he was spotted by an SS man. A burst of machinegun fire raked through Henri's body killing him instantly!

Back in the rabbit hutches, on hearing the machinegun fire that had tragically taken Henri's life, the five remaining survivors decided to pause their attempt to escape. But the inferno around them was becoming unbearable. They knew that they had only one choice, to be burned alive or

Chapter 10: Carnage

to chance escape across the open green, in the likelihood of enduring the same fate as Henri! They remained in the hutches as long as they could bear, but their hair and clothes began to burn. In desperation Robert, Mathieu, Yvon and Clement staggered into the open and raced across the green to the pathway that led to the cemetery, albeit that they were expecting to be gunned-down at any moment. But miraculously they were not spotted by the SS! Somehow the four young men, suffering from bullet wounds, burns and smoke inhalation, managed to stagger along the pathway to the cemetery undetected! They were then able make their escape to the safety of the surrounding countryside. They would each live to tell their tale!

Jean-Marcel Darthout, severely injured and unable to move, remained hidden in the rabbit hutches! He had resigned himself to fate. But fate was to bless him! Miraculously, the inferno had reached its peak and the flames slowly abated. Jean-Marcel, suffering from multiple bullet wounds, burns and choking from smoke inhalation, remained concealed and undetected by the SS! Later on, Jean-Marcel somehow found the strength to crawl from the rabbit hutches to the undergrowth of Armand Senon's garden at the edge of Le Champs de Foire.

There were no other survivors from the Laudy barn. At the Boucholle barn, the Milord Hotel storeroom, the Beaulieu forge, the Denis wine store and the Desourteaux garage, every single man and boy perished by machinegun fire, asphyxiation or by being burned alive. Among the dead were the Mayor, Jean Desourteaux and three of his sons, Etienne the town clerk, Jacques the doctor and Paul the grocer. The mayor's remaining son Hubert, still in hiding near to his garage yard, remained alive, but he

## Chapter 10: Carnage

was reduced to a state of severe shock and mental trauma! Hubert had witnessed a group of thirty or so men and boys being forced into his workshop by the SS. He had then helplessly listened-on as they were systematically shot and incinerated by the soldiers. Fate would have it that Hubert Desourteaux would survive that day. But he was destined never to 'mentally' recover.

The injured footballer, Armand Senon, had managed to remain undetected in his bedroom next to Le Champs de Foire. He had heard shooting and screaming coming from all over the village, and he then saw some soldiers line-up a small group of people against the wall of the nearby Beaulieu forge. He then looked on in horror as the soldiers opened fire with their machine guns, killing the whole group. Armand, in desperation, decided to leave his bedroom and make his way to the trees and undergrowth in his back garden. He later heard the soldiers rummaging through his home before they finally set it alight. As Armand witnessed the smoke and flames sweep through his home, he gripped his wooden crutch determined to attack any SS soldier who might discover him. But the soldiers moved-on, unaware of his concealment in the thick undergrowth of his garden. He then discovered that the badly injured Jean-Marcel Darthout was hiding near to him in the undergrowth. The two young men were aware of each other's presence, but dare not utter a single word in case they were discovered by the soldiers. It would be a long and painful time before they were rescued. But both young men would survive to tell their tales!

Meanwhile, little Roger Godfrin aged just seven years, having bravely evaded the SS soldiers, made his way to the riverbank nearby, but he was horrified when he saw a soldier shoot a small dog. The soldier then spotted Roger and opened fire. But the bullets narrowly missed the child and he quickly jumped into the water! He then swam across the river and concealed himself in the trees and bushes on the opposite bank. Roger remained hidden for what seemed hours, before he finally escaped into the nearby countryside. He eventually found his way to a house just outside the village, when he was given refuge. This brave and spirited child would also live to tell his tale!

The three Jewish children, Jaqueline, Francine and André Pinede remained hidden under the stairwell of the Hotel Avril. They had heard the shooting and had seen the smoke and flames coming from Monsieur Denis's wine store just across the high street. They decided to try to escape through the back garden of the hotel and then make their way across the open countryside; but as they did so they were approached by an SS soldier wielding a rifle. Terrified but keeping a level-head, Jaqueline asked the soldier what was going to happen to them. She was surprised when the soldier answered her in French, urging her and her siblings to run away to the safety of the woodland nearby. The children did not hesitate and made their escape, finally finding refuge in a farmhouse a short distance from the village. It was apparent that there was at least one SS soldier, almost certainly a French-Alsatian conscript, who was prepared to risk his own life in order to save the lives of innocent children. The young soldier's courage and human decency was in stark contrast to his sadistic fellow countryman, Sergeant Georges René Boos, who was only just beginning to prove to his Nazi masters that he was as ruthlessly dependable as any German SS soldier.

## Chapter 10: Carnage

Indeed, Boos was enthusiastically executing his orders elsewhere in the village! Even the most seasoned SS soldiers were appalled at his bloodlust. As one dwelling was burning to the ground, a woman villager made a desperate attempt to escape, but Boos was witnessed by his fellow soldiers pushing the woman back into the building where she was burned alive. At Léopold Boucholle's bakery in the high street, several of the Alsatian soldiers later alleged that they had looked on in horror as Boos forced an infant child into the ovens.

Another ruthless and brutal German SS soldier, Scharführer (Sergeant) Staeger, was witnessed shooting an elderly lady, who was unable to get up from her sickbed. As he did so, the ricochets from the bullets injured one of the French Alsatian soldiers, who was carried away to receive medical treatment at an aid-station on the outskirts of the village.

As the mass-executions in the barns and storehouses were taking place, individual killings were also taking place throughout the village and the surrounding area. What Armand Senon had earlier witnessed from his bedroom window, was an unfortunate group of pedal-cyclists unconnected with Oradour, who had been leisurely riding around the Limosan countryside. As they approached the village, they were apprehended by the SS, who forcibly escorted them to the Beaulieu forge at the entrance to Le Champs de Foire. They were then lined-up against a wall and shot.

The driver of a tram, which was not in public-service, spotted smoke coming from the village as he approached the tram-bridge. He halted the tram and the engineer Marcelin Charlard, got out and approached the SS guards on the bridge. A shot rang out and Marcelin fell fatally wounded to the ground. The driver immediately reversed the tram and returned to Limoges to report the incident. The soldiers threw Marcelin's body from the tram bridge into the river below.

Later that evening, before the transport company in Limoges was able to prevent any further movements, a second tram, laden with passengers, approached the bridge at Oradour. The driver and his passengers were obliviously unaware of the previous incident or of the horror that was still taking place within the village! A soldier halted the tram and ordered everyone to get off. The passengers who were identified as Oradour residents were separated from the others and marched off to what seemed to be some form of command-post on the outskirts of the village. The remaining passengers and the tram-crew were ordered back onto the tram and instructed to return to Limoges.

At the SS command post, the terrified group of Oradour passengers witnessed their village being engulfed in flames. As they watched-on in terrified silence, a long and heated discussion developed between their SS guards, one of whom seemed to be highly distressed and in tears. Suddenly, several of the soldiers raised their rifles and pointed them directly at the passengers as if they were about to open-fire! The incident was abruptly ended by an NCO who ordered the passengers to quickly leave the area and not to return. As they quickly dispersed into the countryside, a soldier offered a young girl the use of a pedal cycle. Another soldier called out to them in French, "You were lucky"! It seemed that at least for some of the SS soldiers, the bloodlust had somewhat abated!

Chapter 11

# The Church

FOLLOWING THE NOISE AND HORROR OF THE murders of the menfolk and boys in the barns and storehouses, another eerie silence gradually fell upon the village. Adolf Diekmann, now turned his attention to the four hundred and fifty or so women and children who had been crammed into the church. Grandmother, Marguerite Rouffanche sat nervously subdued with her daughters and grandson on the benches each side of the aisle. They had heard the shooting and screaming of the men and boys as they were systematically shot and burned in the barns and storerooms nearby and they could smell the smoke and flames billowing from the Hotel Milord storeroom and the Boucholle barn. Suddenly, the main door to the church burst open and two soldiers appeared carrying a heavy wooden box, which they carefully placed near to the altar.

Silence fell upon the women and children as they watched-on in a mixture of fear and curiosity as one of the soldiers set light to a short length of cord which was protruding from the box. The cord began to burn slowly and the soldiers quickly departed; the women and children then heard the church door being secured from outside. A few seconds passed, then smoke and flames began to erupt from the box, followed by a loud explosion. As the thick black smoke spread throughout every part of the church, the terrified women and children were driven to

## Chapter 11: The Church

panic. It was later established that the SS commander had instructed his soldiers to create a device that was capable of asphyxiating every woman and child within the church, using a concoction of loose explosive materials. Indeed, as the toxic fumes engulfed the church, many of the women and children lapsed into unconsciousness. Within the ensuing horror, a small group of women managed to open an internal door to the small vestry adjoining the aisle ... but this desperate act merely delayed their fate; the outside door to the vestry had been secured by the SS.

Two young boys managed to take refuge in the priest's confession box ... the very same confessional that Jean Baptiste Chapelle had provided spiritual comfort to his congregations over many decades. Outside the church door the soldiers listened and waited for the terrified cries within to abate, but the screaming seemed to go on ... endlessly! The attempt to kill the women and children by asphyxiation was happening too slowly for the satisfaction of the SS commander, Adolf Diekmann, so he ordered his troops to quickly finish-off the victims using machine guns.

Utterly terrified, Marguerite Rouffanche and her daughters and grandson, were huddled together desperately gasping for air when the church door suddenly burst open again ... several soldiers then appeared and immediately began to fire their machine guns into the terrified mass of choking women and children. Similarly to their execution method in the Laudy barn, the soldiers then paused to listen for the cries of any survivors, before carrying out a second wave of intense gun fire. This was followed by a hail of hand grenades thrown indiscriminately amongst the women, children, infants and babies. As this act of barbarism took place, a soldier discovered the two young boys who were hiding in the confession box ... they were immediately dispatched by pistol shots to the head. The soldiers then began to pile together any combustible materials they could find within the church, such as seats, cushions and benches; which they then set alight before quickly departing. They again secured the church door from the outside as they did so.

Miraculously, Marguerite Rouffanche somehow remained alive, but she was suffering badly from smoke inhalation; she had witnessed the deaths of her daughters and grandson and she had been rendered to a devastating state of shock and despair! But just like Robert Hébras in the Laudy barn, the overwhelming desire to survive instinctively drove Marguerite to seek a means of escape. Trapped within the smoke and flames, Marguerite could see sunlight beaming through the three glass Norman windows above the altar; somehow she got a foothold below the windows and heaved herself upwards. She then frantically punched at the leaded-glass until it began to give way; but the outside of the window was protected by an iron mesh screen. With almost super-human strength, Marguerite pushed and punched at the mesh until it gave-way! She then propelled herself through the window, and in doing so, she fell heavily on to the grass slope some ten feet below.

Marguerite somehow managed to get to her feet, but she then saw a young woman, Henriette Joyeux holding her baby son René, appear in the window above! In desperation Henriette threw down baby René to Marguerite, but she could not catch the boy and he fell onto the steep grass slope below the window. Henriette then jumped from the window, hitting the ground heavily. At this point, a soldier

## Chapter 11: The Church

appeared and began to shoot at the women with his machine gun ... both women and the baby were riddled with bullets. Henriette and baby René died on the spot; but Marguerite managed to stagger to the back of the churchyard, where she concealed herself in a vegetable garden.

Grandmother Marguerite Rouffange, suffering from multiple bullet wounds, shock and smoke-inhalation and close to death, lay there for the next twenty four hours. She was the sole survivor of the four hundred and fifty women and children who had been asphyxiated, shot, mutilated by hand grenades and then burned alive within the holy walls of the ancient Church of Saint Martin ... but she would live to tell her tale!

As Marguerite lay there in the vegetable garden, the church, already engulfed by smoke and fire, became a raging inferno! The bell tower was acting like a huge chimney drawing the flames upwards and through the roof. The heat was so intense that the old cast-bronze church bell began to melt and then fell heavily onto the floor below. As the flames roared, a young SS officer, Untersturmführer (Second Lieutenant) Knug, ventured too near to the burning church, presumably in an act of morbid curiosity ... his folly was rewarded by a falling roof tile which struck him to the ground. Second Lieutenant Knug was destined to be the only SS fatality in Oradour that day; his family would later be formally notified that he had died fighting honourably for Germany. Curiously, Sergeant Georges René Boos was subsequently ordered to drive the fatally injured Knug to a hospital in Limoges. It is not known why Boos in particular was ordered to carry out this task; but it is possible that his monstrous conduct was deemed to be too excessive even by SS standards?

CHAPTER 12

# Despair

AS THE CHURCH AND THE OTHER EXECUTION SITES were being engulfed by flames, Adolf Diekmann ordered his troops to begin the final phase of his 'search' operation at Oradour-sur-Glane. He ordered that the remaining buildings were to be thoroughly searched and any survivors were to be shot; on completion of the searches, every building was to be burned to the ground without exception. The company commander, Otto Khan with military efficiency, deployed his troops throughout the village. The soldiers went about their odious task promptly and efficiently ... taking every opportunity to loot anything of value.

Oradour-sur-Glane was not a small village; it consisted of hundreds of dwellings, hotels, cafes, shops, schools, storehouses, garages, barns and agricultural buildings. To thoroughly search and destroy the whole village would take many more hours. Otto Khan therefore judged that it would be necessary to leave a platoon of some thirty soldiers in the village overnight to finalise the operation. The large, well-stocked home of the Dupic family was selected as a suitable base for the soldiers remaining overnight. The household provided an abundant wine cellar and plenty of good food ready for the taking; the SS could complete their mass-murder operation with full bellies and a comfortable berth. The Dupic home was destined to be the very last building in the ancient village to be destroyed. As the small contingent of soldiers settled-down for the night at the Dupic abode, Major Diekmann, Captain Khan and Second Lieutenant Barth departed from the village with the main convoy to their next destination, the small town of Nieul, some 10 miles away. The SS soldiers were later seen by the town's folk of Nieul, sharing out the cash and other property that they had stolen from Oradour.

Earlier that afternoon, the people in the nearby villages and farms had seen the SS convoy as it had approached Oradour; they had heard the gunshots and explosions and could now see the smoke and fire as it swept through the village. Many of the people in these outlying areas had family and friends who had gone shopping in Oradour, but had not yet returned. Many had young children who had gone to the schools during the morning. Throughout the afternoon and evening desperate parents had tried to approach the SS guards, but were aggressively turned away. One parent, Madame Demery, who knew the surrounding countryside well, managed to sneak through the SS cordon and entered the boy's school, which she found to be deserted? She frantically searched for her young sons, but all she found were the children's school bags still hanging in the classroom! Clearly the children had departed from the school in quite a hurry? She could hear the shouts of the soldiers nearby and fearing that she would be discovered, she managed to return home undetected by the SS; but the fear remained ... where were the children?

Later in the evening, Professor Aimé Forest, a refugee parent temporarily residing nearby, spoke to the SS

## Chapter 12: Despair

guards at the tram bridge. Despite being warned to leave, he bravely insisted on speaking to someone in authority; eventually he was approached by a French-speaking soldier. Professor Forest explained that his sons, Michel and Dominique, had not returned home and he believed that they were somewhere in the village. The soldier assured him that the children were in a place of safety; but the professor was then instructed to leave immediately or he would be shot!

As night time arrived, Robert Hébras and Mathieu Borie, who had survived the massacre at the Laudy barn, managed to take refuge in the home of Monsieur Barataud in the hamlet of Martinier, a short distance from the village. Robert was in a poor physical state, suffering from gun-shot wounds, burns and smoke inhalation. Coincidentally, the three Jewish Pinede children, had also managed to escape to the same house; Jaqueline, the oldest girl, assisted in dressing the wounds and burns sustained by Robert. In their places of relative safety, the young survivors now began to reflect on the fate of their families and loved-ones. Robert was confident that his father, who had been working outside the village had probably sought refuge at some other homestead; but what of his mother and his two sisters, Georgette and little Denise, whom he had last seen being herded away to the church earlier that afternoon?

Jaqueline and Francine Pinede knew that their parents had assembled with the other villagers at Le Champs de Foire; had the SS discovered that they were Jews and taken them away to be deported to a concentration camp? Jean-Marcel Darthout, still concealed in the burning ruins near to Le Champs de Foire, had last seen his young

## Chapter 12: Despair

wife Angéle and his mother, being marched off to the church earlier that afternoon ... surely they were alive and safe within the protection of its holy walls?

During the night, fragmented information of what was happening at Oradour began to circulate around the surrounding communities and farm houses. Nobody dared to approach the burning village as it was known that some of the SS soldiers had remained there overnight. But the desperate need to discover the fate of their loved-ones, particularly the children, was overwhelming. Anxiously the distraught parents and local residents waited throughout the long night for the remaining soldiers to leave the village. As dawn broke, the SS soldiers committed their final act of destruction at Oradour, setting light to Monsieur Dupic's house, before finally boarding their trucks and departing from the village. The murderous orgy of death and destruction was complete.

Cautiously, the parents and surviving villagers approached and entered the smoking ruins. People went directly to their homes or to the places where they hoped to find their children and loved-ones. But hopes of finding anyone alive began to fade as they discovered that every single building had been destroyed! As they frantically searched the smouldering ruins, the charred remains of the men and boys were found in the barns and storehouses; the bullet-riddled body of Henri Poutaraud was discovered on the cemetery pathway.

But what of the women and children, surely not even the SS could not have been so monstrous as to harm them? It was clear that the SS had succeeded in massacring most of the menfolk, but it seemed inconceivable to the peaceful

Chapter 12: Despair

villagers that any harm could have come to the women and children ... but where had they been taken? The stark reality of Adolf Deikmann's depraved and monstrous 'search' operation had yet to be fully comprehended!

The surviving villagers' dilemma was brutally ended when a group of parents and other local people approached the smouldering ruins of the church; the roof and spire had collapsed and they noted that the protective iron mesh over the Norman windows had been forced outwards? As they entered the church, the horrific vision that was presented to them must have been impossible to grasp! The smell of burned flesh and smouldering woodwork was overbearing. The blackened and scorched remains of the women and children were strewn throughout the church; very few of the bodies were identifiable; most had been burned beyond recognition. It became immediately obvious what had taken place; hundreds of shell cases from the machine guns were scattered over the church floor; the marble altar and memorial plaques had been blasted into fragments by gunfire and explosives. The heat generated by the fire in the bell-tower had been so intense that the ancient bronze bell had melted and fallen onto the stone flooring below. Curiously, the wooden confession box was undamaged; but when it was opened, the bodies of two young boys were discovered. The SS had found the boys hiding in the confessional during the 'mopping-up' procedures and had murdered both children by pistol-shots to the head.

During the following long hours, the young mechanic Robert Hébras and the stone mason Mathieu Borie, together with the other survivors of the Laudy barn, pensively awaited news of their loved-ones; likewise the

Jewish Pinede children and little Roger Godfrin. The injured footballer Armand Senon, brothers Maurice and Joseph Beaubreuil, Paul Doutre and Hubert Desourteaux the garage owner: all awaited the inevitable news of the horrifying fate of their families and loved-ones!

Chapter 13

# Survivors

WHAT THE SS DID NOT TAKE INTO CONSIDERATION when they carried out the mass-murders of the women and children in the church, was the sheer determination of Marguerite Rouffanche to survive! It was not until the Sunday afternoon, nearly 24 hours after the massacre, that faint cries were heard coming from the vegetable patch near to the churchyard! Marguerite's rescuers could hardly recognise her; she was covered with garden soil and blood from her multiple bullet wounds; she was suffering from blood-loss, burns, smoke inhalation and mental trauma ... but she was alive and able to tell her rescuers everything that had happened! The premeditated and murderous intent of the SS soldiers to murder all of the women and children within the church was now clearly beyond any reasonable doubt!

As the local populace became confident that the SS had finally departed from the village, so more and more people began to return. There was a desperation by parents to find their children; but they would soon discover that there was little hope of finding them alive. Those who ventured into the church were confronted with the nightmare reality of the massacre; parents searched desperately among the charred and mutilated remains for items of clothing or small toys that might identify their children; but most were burned beyond recognition. The villagers searched the homes, shops, hotels, schools and other buildings for missing relatives and friends; but hope of finding anyone alive was getting more and more unlikely. The macabre discovery of the bodies of the two boys in the confessional and the remains of the infant child in the bakery oven, must have been utterly beyond the comprehension of the traumatised villagers.

From time to time hopes were reignited, particularly when it became known that little Roger Godfrin and the Pinede children and the five survivors of the Laudy barn were alive. Hubert Desourteaux, the garage owner emerged from his workshop yard mentally traumatised but alive! Paul Doutre, who had remained hidden in his garden shed, also emerged. Brothers Maurice and Joseph Beaubreuil had remained concealed in their aunt's house and then escaped into the surrounding countryside. Armand Senon hobbled on his wooden crutch from the undergrowth of his garden near to Le Champs de Foire, accompanied by Jean-Marcel Darthout. Suffering from multiple bullet wounds, burns and smoke inhalation, Jean-Marcel had miraculously crawled from the burning rabbit hutches and somehow made his way to Armand's garden!

During the following hours and days, the villagers and the wider population of the area, gradually grasped the full scale and barbaric nature of the massacre! Alongside the chaos and despair, there developed a passionate determination to attain justice! It was obvious that the SS, even by their standards, had committed a massively grotesque crime at Oradour-sur-Glane. But in the Limosan region, the civil authorities and the Gendarmerie remained under the direct control of the

Vichy Government ... the subservient puppets of the occupying Germans!

The brutal nature of the German occupation of France and the countless atrocities that had taken place throughout the country were already a matter of record, but the people of Oradour realised that the death and destruction in their village had elevated the crimes of the SS in France to an unprecedented level. The surviving citizens of Oradour and the surrounding communities had a burning desire for justice, but who could they turn to? Who could they trust to carry out a major war-crime investigation? As ever, their instinct was to turn to the Church for guidance.

Word of the massacre was quickly relayed to the Bishop of Limoges, Monseigneur Rastouil. The Bishop guessed that following the Allied Invasion, the German authorities were coming to terms with the fact that they were probably going to lose the war and would be held to account for their crimes! But Monseigneur Rastouil also realised that the SS would make every effort to conceal and discredit any accusations made against them; he therefore advised local officials to carry-out their investigations in great secrecy, emphasising the dangers involved should their activities be discovered by the Germans. The SS in particular, would have no qualms in the elimination of witnesses! The investigation would therefore have to be carried out on a 'need to know' basis!

A war-crime investigation of this magnitude would normally require the highest levels of experience and expertise of professional policing organisations, but in the present circumstances this was impossible; the Church and the Red Cross, assisted by trusted health officials and local volunteers, would have to do their best! The Church authorities also took on the heavy burden of providing much of the medical care, hygiene facilities and providing temporary homes for the displaced survivors and their families. They also conscientiously attended to their primary duty of spiritual support to the ever growing numbers of emotionally traumatised men, women and children; and all whilst carefully ensuring that they did not attract the attention of the Germans or the Vichy authorities!

Although the newspapers and radio stations remained very much under the control and censorship of the Germans and the Vichy government, many French journalists were determined to establish the truth; but the gathering and recording of evidence proved to be extremely difficult for both the journalists and the investigators. To avoid detection from the SS, important items of evidence and documentation were secretly buried each night in discreet locations. Sanitising the scene of the massacre proved to be extremely distressing for the clergy and their helpers; it was mid-summer and there were hundreds of rapidly decomposing corpses strewn throughout the village. Most of the bodies were burned beyond recognition, but every effort was made to identify each victim, before covertly arranging burial procedures.

Means of transportation of the bodies were limited to wooden hand carts; doors were removed from the smouldering ruins and utilised as stretchers. Hundreds of bed-sheets and blankets were used to cover the corpses in order to shield the sheer horror that prevailed throughout the village. By necessity, this distressing but vital function, was carried-out with stealth and with the utmost urgency!

The Bishop's predictions regarding an attempted cover-up by the Germans proved to be correct; just as the investigators were beginning their onerous tasks, several trucks carrying SS troops returned to the village! On hearing the approach of the soldiers, the clergy and their helpers quickly scattered into the surrounding countryside. However, the small number of SS troops did not have the facilities nor time to cover-up their crime. They manage to dig several pits and then buried some of the bodies; but concealing such a massive atrocity proved impossible. The soldiers gave up their efforts and departed from the village later that day; leaving the scene of the massacre mostly intact. The investigators and volunteer helpers then cautiously returned to the village to continue to gather the evidence, in the full knowledge that their lives could well be in peril! It was later learned that one of the SS soldiers who had returned with the 'cleaning-up' party, was none other than the fanatical French Alsatian volunteer, George René Boos!

Very much aware that he was putting his life in jeopardy, Monseigneur Rastouil, protested in the strongest terms to the officer in command of the regular German army in Limoges, General Gleiniger. The General was indeed appalled by the abhorrent crime of the SS at Oradour, and he ensured that knowledge of the massacre reached the highest levels of the German command. Indeed, none other than Field Marshall Irwin Rommel ordered Heinz Lammerding to carry out a full military enquiry, with a view to court-marshalling any SS officers who were involved in the massacre. Whether Rommel was aware that Lammerding himself was implicated, is a matter of conjecture! In the months that followed, during the volatile retreat of the German forces from France, General Gleiniger was apprehended by the SS. It was subsequently reported that he had committed suicide ... but it is probable that he was murdered by his vengeful SS captors. Bishop Rastouil was also arrested by the SS, but mercifully he was later released.

Inevitably, the battles that were taking place in Normandy completely overshadowed the horrors that had taken place at Oradour. As Das Reich continued their journey towards the Allied landing-beaches some 260 miles to the north of Oradour, they were constantly harassed and delayed by vengeful Resistance fighters. When the division eventually arrived at Normandy it was too late ... the Allies had consolidated their beach-heads and were now battling their way inland.

Ironically, Adolf Diekmann, the architect of the murders, was killed a few days later during the heavy fighting that took place in Normandy ... as were many of the soldiers who had committed the massacre at Oradour. Second Lieutenant Heinz Barth, the seasoned killer of civilians in Russia, Czechoslovakia and Oradour, was seriously wounded, losing a leg in the fighting; but he survived and eventually returned to Germany for rehabilitation. The fanatical Alsatian, Sergeant Georges Boos, was captured by the Allies and incarcerated in a POW camp in England, where he would remain for the duration of the war. Captain Otto Khan survived the fighting in Normandy, but lost his left arm in a later battle in Czechoslovakia; he was finally was captured by the Russians, but was later released to return to his home in Germany.

Meanwhile, in the smouldering ruins of Oradour-

## Chapter 13: Survivors

sur-Glane, the volunteer investigators stealthily continued with their evidence-gathering. Eventually, as the Germans retreated from France and the hated Vichy Government were overthrown, the Gendarmerie were trusted to take over the investigation. Marguerite Rouffange, Robert Hébras and the other survivors, having made their statements to the authorities, had no choice but to mourn their murdered loved ones and to get on with their lives ... but many years would pass before any of the SS killers would be brought to justice.

CHAPTER 14

# Peace?

AS THE SMOULDERING REMAINS OF THE ONCE peaceful and vibrant village of Oradour-sur-Glane finally cooled, 'Mother' France was in the process of being liberated by the western Allies. The following year, Peace finally came to a ravaged world. New hopes and dreams could be envisaged ... a 'new' world, a more tolerant world, would be created under the helm of the newly formed United Nations!

But there were scores to be settled! Perhaps too many scores? Nazi atrocities numbered in their thousands; the victims of their crimes were numbered in tens of millions! Could justice ever be achieved for all those victims? Nazi Germany would be made to answer for their atrocities! Indeed, the top Nazis were either already dead or had been apprehended and were awaiting trial in Nuremburg.

But what of the tens of thousands of war criminals still at large? What of the one hundred and fifty or so SS soldiers who murdered the men, women and children of Oradour-sur-Glane? Major Adolf Diekmann was dead; half of his head blown away near the Normandy beaches! But what of Captain Otto Khan and Second Lieutenant Heinz Barth and Sergeant Georges René Boos and many other of the SS soldiers believed to be still alive ... somewhere in war-torn Europe! Surely it would not be too difficult to track these soldiers down?

There was an abundance of captured German military records that could assist investigators in piecing together the evidence necessary to locate, apprehend and convict the perpetrators? Thanks to the Bishop of Limoges, the raw evidence at the scene of the massacre at Oradour had been secretly gathered in anticipation of a major war-crime investigation!

And what of the senior German officers implicated in this monstrous crime? What of Field Marshall Hugo Sperrle, who signed the so-called anti-terrorist counter-measures orders, which gave Adolf Diekmann the confidence to commit his crimes? What of General Heinz Lammerding, who allegedly ordered the search operation at Oradour? From the top Nazis downwards, the two main excuses for their crimes were that they were either unaware of what was happening, or if the evidence against them was damning ... they were simply obeying orders from a higher authority. They had all taken the oath of absolute obedience to their leader! In effect, within their autocratic Nazi regime, all blame could be pushed 'upstairs' to their Fuhrer, Adolf Hitler, who was now conveniently dead!

To the credit of the victorious Allies, radical new international laws, specifically framed to convict suspected war criminals, were promptly enacted. No matter what the status or nationality of the perpetrator, the new laws, in theory, provided the ability for investigators and courts of law to bring offenders to justice. But the thousands of war-crimes investigators throughout Europe, were faced with unprecedented numbers of major and serious crimes: Crimes against Humanity, waging Aggressive war, Violation of the customs of war and Conspiracy to commit these offences! Which particular crimes took precedence over others? Compared to the major war-crimes such as the Holocaust, Oradour's plight for justice fell within the category of countless other serious war crimes. Within the devastated wastelands of Europe, the numbers of investigators, lawyers, judges and judicial administrative staff and resources, were all extremely limited!

International politics had an enormous influence upon which particular enquiries had priority of resources. The priority of the United Nations was to retain and consolidate the hard-earned Peace. None of the Allies wished to repeat the mistakes which had led to Nazi Germany's rise to power; the prospect of Germany ever again falling under the control of extremists was unthinkable! The Nazis leaders of course were to be punished; the war-criminals were to be punished. But it was vital that the Nation of Germany and its people should be rebuilt in-line with the peaceful and democratic aspirations of the 'new' Europe!

The Americans, the British and the French were only too aware that to repeat the same punishing reparations placed upon an already devastated Germany, as they did following the Great War, would be a monumental mistake! The whole extremist cycle of German politics would be reborn! This view was not echoed by the Russians, who wanted to take-over all of Germany and then go on to occupy the rest of Europe! Stalin's aspirations for justice amounted to summarily executing all Nazis and subjugating Europe to his brand of Communism. The fear of a Russian dictatorship of Europe was as abhorrent to the western Allies as the fascist empire created by Hitler!

So how did world-wide politics affect the justice that

was craved by the relatives and friends of the 642 victims of the atrocity at Oradour-sur-Glane? The new President of France, General Charles de Gaulle, was an astute and pragmatic politician. Following the war he knew that his country had been deeply divided by Petain's Vichy Government. The people of the Limosan, particularly the survivors of Oradour, sought prompt justice and revenge against the Germans; but de Gaulle knew that the likelihood of achieving quick-justice was remote. He was also concerned that as time passed, the memory of Oradour's plight might fade; he therefore took the decision to make a very public and formal visit to the village.

During the final weeks of the war in Europe, on the cold and clear afternoon of Sunday 4th March 1945, Charles de Gaulle solemnly walked amongst the ruins of the village; he appeared visibly shaken and there was a look of cold determination on his face. Immediately following his visit, he ordered that the ruins of Oradour-sur-Glane were to be preserved for all time, thereby ensuring that the victims and the crimes that took place there were never to be forgotten. Without doubt, de Gaulle's decision retained political and judicial importance to the massacre; the story of Oradour-sur-Glane would be forever enshrined within its bleak ruins! The French government went on to appoint a comprehensive team of war-crime investigators to continue with the search and apprehension of the SS soldiers who had committed the atrocity ... but another nine years would slowly pass before any trial took place!

CHAPTER 15

# Time Passes

MARGUERITE ROUFFANGE MADE A SLOW BUT miraculous recovery. As her bullet wounds healed and her trauma and grief was gradually stabilised, the 'martyred' village of Oradour-sur-Glane had become a sombre hive of activity. The French authorities went about their sensitive work of preserving the ruins in line with General de Gaulle's directive. Nearby, the first buildings of the 'new' town of Oradour-sur-Glane began to arise. Marguerite would make the new Oradour her home for the rest of her long life!

During the final months of the war, young Robert Hébras, following a brief period of recovery from his burns and bullet wounds, joined the ranks of the French army; he was determined to fight the Germans to the last! He then returned to his peace-time work as a mechanic, taking up residence in the town of St Junien, just eight miles from Oradour.

The other survivors of the Laudy barn Jean-Marcel Darthout, Yvon Roby, Clement Broussaudier and stonemason Mathieu Borie, also settled back to 'normality'. Likewise Maurice and Joseph Beaubreuil, who had hidden in their aunt's house. And Armand Senon, the injured footballer. And Paul Doutre, who had hidden in his home until it was burned by the soldiers. And the Jewish Pinede children. They all survived, but their lives could never be the same.

Little Roger Godfrin, the plucky refugee child who had courageously evaded the SS soldiers during the long hours of the massacre, orphaned and alone, returned to his native town of Charly, hundreds of miles to the North in the Lorraine region adjoining the Alsace.

But this small band of survivors, whilst pragmatically getting on with their new, peaceful lives, all retained a burning desire for justice. They prepared themselves for the day when they would be called to tell their stories and to witness justice being placed upon the soldiers who had destroyed their homes and murdered their loved-ones. But when would that day come? The Gendarmerie, in liaison with a multitude of international war-crimes investigating agencies, were diligently pursuing both German and French-Alsatian SS soldiers suspected of committing the massacre, ... but the years continued to pass!

The world was rapidly moving-on. Above all, the people of Europe wanted Peace and Reconciliation. But a new 'Cold War' between the Eastern and Western powers had transpired ... and both sides now had 'weapons of mass destruction'! A devastated and divided Germany sat right on the front-line between the 'new' enemy, Russia, and the Western European and American super-powers! World peace was again on a knife's-edge! The West German nation were now our new friends and allies; the country was in the process of being rebuilt and 'rehabilitated'!

The new democratic West German government was as committed to the elimination of Nazism as the western Allies. The denazification of government departments and major businesses was enthusiastically and swiftly carried out; but it remained apparent that many thousands of the officials in these organisations, including the police, had previously been members of the Nazi party or had carried out Nazi policies and doctrine! Of these officials, many could be attributed to have been 'war-criminals' simply because they were carrying out their 'lawful' terms of employment!

Inevitably, in order to rebuild the nation's vital infrastructure, a pragmatic solution to retain essential officials was settled upon. War-crime investigations would continue, but only on the basis that cases against individuals were of the most serious nature and could be proven 'beyond reasonable doubt'. An insurmountable back-log of investigations transpired! Amongst the ranks of officialdom within the West German government departments and private businesses, were thousands ex-SS officers and soldiers, including the likes of Heinz Lammerding, commander of the brutal Das Reich division, together with many of his subordinates ... among them Captain Otto Khan, the company commander of the soldiers who carried out the massacre at Oradour!

After the major war-crimes trials in Nuremberg, Russia's leader, Joseph Stalin had been very disappointed by the 'leniency' shown to many of the defendants. His heart had never been committed to these 'show-case' trials ... if he had had his way, he would have simply purged the whole Nazi regime! In East Germany, the occupying Russians had already apprehended and summarily executed hundreds of Nazi officials and SS officers; or had conveniently re-employed them, if it suited their needs! Just like in the West, many ex-Nazis and SS soldiers were 'hiding in plain sight', including Heinz Barth, the brutal Untersturmführer who had commanded the firing squads in the villages of Czechoslovakia and at Oradour-sur-Glane! He had since married, had children and was peacefully pursuing a new career in the town of Gransee in Communist East Germany ... many decades would pass before justice caught-up with Heinz Barth!

Nevertheless, the French police together with the other investigative agencies continued to search for the 'killers of Oradour'. Gradually the locations of individual surviving SS officers, NCOs and soldiers, suspected of the crime, were discovered. One of the first to be apprehended was Sergeant Georges René Boos; he had remained in captivity in England as a prisoner of war and on repatriation, was re-arrested pending trial by the French military authorities. During the following years, the identities of over sixty Germans and French-Alsatians, suspected of committing the massacre, were discovered throughout Europe and further afield in the modern day country of Vietnam; previously the French colony of Indo China.

An unsuccessful attempt was made to extradite General Heinz Lammerding, who was now known to be a prosperous businessman residing in Düsseldorf. But it appeared that there was insufficient evidence to convince the West German and Anglo-American legal authorities of his guilt; Lammerding also took steps to temporarily lay-low until interest in his culpability subdued! Eventually, having received legal advice, Lammerding sent a written statement to the French investigators denying any guilt ... but they were not to be put-off and made preparations for him to be tried *'in absentia'*.

Curiously, the whereabouts of Captain Otto Khan, also

living openly in West Germany, was not discovered until the 1960s. He was never brought to trial for war-crimes, albeit that the French also prepared charges against him to be tried *'in absentia'*. Indeed, of the sixty-plus surviving suspects, forty four ex-SS soldiers, both German and French-Alsatians, were destined to be tried in this way!

CHAPTER 16

# The Bordeaux Trial

ON A COLD JANUARY MORNING IN 1953, A pathetically small number of ex-SS soldiers, twenty one in total, appeared before a military court in the French city of Bordeaux, some 120 miles from Oradour. The population of France were still recoiling from the thousands of SS war crimes that had occurred throughout their country during the German occupation; particularly those major atrocities carried out by the Das Reich division at Tulle and Oradour-sur-Glane … Anger and resentment were still very raw! Although nine years had passed since the massacre, many of the defendants were still in their twenties; they had been teenagers when they had, allegedly, committed their crimes! Only seven of the SS defendants were German … the other fourteen were French-Alsatians! But where were the rest of the 150 or so soldiers that took part? Where were their leaders? Where were the senior Nazi officers who had allegedly ordered the atrocity? Nine years of investigations and only twenty one low-ranking troops had been traced and brought before the court!

From the very beginning, the political nature of the trial came to the fore. Why were the Frenchmen being tried alongside the German soldiers? Surely it was the Germans who were the enemy and perpetrators of the crime? The French-Alsatians had been forcibly conscripted and had participated in the killings at pain of death, if they had defied their orders? However, the somewhat lame excuse of "I was only obeying orders" had been used by too many German war criminals, at too many trials, since the end of the war. But these particular defendants were Frenchmen being held to justice before a French court!

This controversial conundrum was further exacerbated by the very nature of one of the French defendants ... before the court stood George René Boos, the 'monster' French-Alsatian SS volunteer, who allegedly bullied his fellow countrymen to kill defenceless men, women and children! Boos, who had allegedly pushed a woman into a burning building to suffer a slow and agonising death! Boos, who had allegedly burned an infant child to death in the ovens of the village bakery!

The survivors of Oradour and their relatives and friends, demanded that all of the soldiers should be tried together; no matter what their nationality. They should all stand accused of the same crimes! But this sentiment was not shared by the people of northern France, particularly in the Alsace and Lorraine regions. They were generally supportive of the young French SS conscripts, advocating that they had been 'forced' by the Germans to commit their crimes: they had no choice ... they were 'obeying orders' given to them by their brutal and uncompromising Nazi masters! The Press named this sorry group the *Malgré-nous*, meaning: 'against our will'.

It is emphasised that the trial at Bordeaux was a military tribunal. Military courts were conducted on a similar basis to civilian criminal hearings, however, such trials were presided over by military officers. In order to ensure that the legal complexities of the trial were carried out correctly, a senior civilian judge was appointed as the 'presiding' officer. For this particular trial, Judge Marcel Nussy Saint-Saëns was selected; he was an able and experienced legislator and well-suited to deal with the complex emotional, political and legal issues that were destined to arise throughout the trial.

One of the first and most important of the political issues was promptly cleared-up by Nussy Saint-Saëns: the defendants would all stand trial together no matter what their nationality ... German or French! The scene was set for much controversy to follow! The relationship between the peoples of the southern French region of the Limosan and the northern regions of the Alsace and Lorraine was destined to become highly strained for decades to come!

After nine years of investigations, what actual evidence existed that was likely to secure the convictions of the SS soldiers for the war-crimes at Oradour? Well the physical evidence was overwhelming! A whole village and its 642 murdered residents, burned to the ground ... but preserved for the World to see! Captured German military records clearly identified the SS Das Reich division as the perpetrators. But Das Reich consisted of up to 19,000 soldiers; which particular soldiers carried out the crime? General Heinz Lammerding, the division commander, who allegedly ordered the 'search' operation at Oradour, was known to be alive and well and living in Germany; why was he not arrested and brought to the court in Bordeaux to stand trial with the other German defendants? And what of Captain Otto Khan and Second Lieutenant Heinz Barth? These were the officers who allegedly assisted Adolf Diekmann in planning the massacre, and then went on to command the systematic mass-murder of innocent men, women and children? They were believed to be alive and living somewhere in Germany; why had they not been pursued, arrested and brought before the court to stand trial with the other defendants?

Not one single SS officer stood in the dock! The only non-commissioned officers present were Sergeant Georges René Boos and a rather unremarkable Oberscharführer (Sergeant-Major), Karl Lenz who, just a few months prior to the massacre, had been transferred from the defunct Luftwaffe to make up the dwindling numbers of the Das Reich division!

It was not only the small number of ex-SS soldiers present that was of obvious dissatisfaction; the actual court-room at Bordeaux was also much too small! The defendants sat squashed together closely surrounded by gendarmes, lawyers, court officials, press reporters and the representatives of the survivors and their families; all closely hemmed-in by as many members of the public as could be squeezed into the building! Looking down upon the confusing and crowded courtroom, sat Judge Marcel Nussy Saint-Saëns and his 'bench' of military presiding officers.

In the small and compacted area of the courtroom allocated to the defendants, the ex-SS soldiers separated themselves in two groups. The Frenchmen were determined to distance themselves from the Germans; presumably to demonstrate to the court that they did not wish to be associated with their former military masters ... they considered themselves to be *victims* of the Germans, not the perpetrators of the crimes they had been forced to commit! It was curious to note that

Georges René Boos, although a French-Alsatian, chose to sit with the Germans; presumably because he may have felt intimidated by the hostile attitude that his fellow countrymen had shown towards him ... or perhaps he may have considered himself to be more German than French?

Oberscharführer Karl Lenz, like Boos had been held in captivity since the end of the war. As the senior non-commissioned officer, he was of obvious interest to the prosecutors. At the time of the massacre, Lenz was 29 years of age and his rank indicated that he would have held considerable responsibility and knowledge of the SS 'search' operation at Oradour; however, it was clear from the evidence given by the other soldiers, that Lenz had been a figure of insignificance and ridicule. As a recent transferee from the Luftwaffe, Lenz was not as feared nor held in such great esteem as the more battle-hardened SS soldiers.

When questioned, Lenz admitted to the court that he had been present at Oradour, but prior to arriving at the village he had an argument with Captain Khan, who subsequently ordered him to remain outside of the village on sentry duties. He said that having little else to do, he climbed up a tree where he spent some of his time observing the local landscape and playing with a stray dog. He went on to say that he had never at any time entered the village and that he did not participate in, nor witness, any of the atrocities that took place. Despite considerable cross-examination by the prosecutor, he did not waver from this story; but it seemed incredulous that Lenz, who as a boy had been in the Hitler Youth and in 1938 joined the Luftwaffe, attaining the highest level of 'non-commissioned' rank, would not have held significant authority throughout the whole 'operation'. Needless to say, his account was regarded with considerable speculation and doubt by the court!

When Scharführer Georges René Boos came to the witness box, like many of the defendants, he appeared to possess a very selective recollection of the massacre; although he did admit to being 'involved' in the executions of the men and boys at Hubert Desourteaux's garage and at the Beaulieu forge ... but he stressed that he and the other soldiers, had been acting on the direct orders of the company commander, Otto Khan. Despite accusations made by several soldiers, Boos denied any knowledge of the murder of the infant child in the bakery oven and also denied forcing a woman into a burning building and throwing hand grenades at the women and children inside the church.

It seemed the other defendants, particularly the French-Alsatians, were very keen to deflect the worst accusations towards Boos, who they clearly disliked and regarded as a traitor. Boos went on to confirm to the court that he had later been ordered to drive the fatally injured Untersturmführer Knug to the hospital in Limoges. He said the reason he had been selected for this task was because he was a trained 'medic'. He went on to say that after he had left Knug at the hospital, he had immediately returned to Oradour.

The only other soldiers holding non-commissioned officer ranks were both Germans:

Wilhelm Bläschke, German, Scharführer, Sergeant
Wilhelm Boehme, German, Rottenfurhrer, Corporal

The other defendants were classed as private soldiers:

Herbert Daab, German, SS-Mann
Erwin Dagenhardt, German, SS-Mann
Herman Frenzel, German, SS-Mann
Fritz Pfeufer, German, SS-Mann
Joseph Busch, French, SS-Mann
Albert Daul, French, SS-Mann
Jean-Pierre Elsässer, French, SS-Mann
Fernand Giedinger, French, SS-Mann
Paul Graff, French, SS-Mann
Camille Grienenberger, French, SS-Mann
Louis Hoelinger, French, SS-Mann
Antoine Lohner, French, SS-Mann
Jean Niess, French, SS-Mann
Albert Ochs, French, SS-Mann
Louis Prestel, French, SS-Mann
Alfred Spaeth, French, SS-Mann
Henri Weber, French, SS-Mann

Prior to the trial, a German SS-Mann, Wilhelm Nobbe, was found to be 'clinically insane' and was judged to be unfit to appear before the court.

As each of the defendants stood up to tell their stories, it was clear from the start that most of them, just like Karl Lenz, were either lying or were giving the court only 'selective' recollections of their involvement in the massacre. This type of defence had been frequently used at numerous war-crime trials after the war and as a result, the French had promptly enacted a new law of 'Collective Responsibility'. This legislation implied that: 'if you were there, then you must have participated in the crime, the onus is on you to prove your innocence'! To add to this, in 1945 the Allied legislators at Nuremberg had directed that the SS was a 'criminal' organisation, and as such all members of the SS were criminals. The defendants at Bordeaux were therefore deemed to be war criminals before the trial had even begun! Nevertheless, Judge Nussy Saint-Saëns went out of his way to ensure that the defendants were treated with respect and given every legal support throughout the trial ... but the odds were very much against them!

The German defendants, Fritz Pfeufer and Herman Frenzel, admitted that they, and other soldiers, had machine-gunned the men and boys in Hubert Desourteaux's garage, but like Georges Boos, they said they were acting under the direct orders of Otto Khan. The Frenchman Antoine Lohner, said that he saw Georges Boos shoot two women near to the church and had also witnessed Boos and Scharführer Staeger, throwing hand grenades into the church. Earlier, Lohner had also accused Karl Lenz of throwing grenades into the church, but when further questioned, he admitted that he had been mistaken, and that it had been another soldier, 'not present at the trial'. Inevitably, there were accusations and counter-accusations made by many of the defendants throughout the trial and the court was forced to treat their evidence with cautious speculation.

Another Frenchman, Albert Ochs, said that he had been present when Scharführer Staeger had machine-gunned an elderly lady in her home. Ochs said that he had been injured in the legs by the ricochets of the bullets, and that he had spent the rest of the day at an aid-station outside of the village. The German, Herbert Daab, said he

## Chapter 16: The Bordeaux Trial

had been present in a barn where a group of men and boys were executed; he stated that he had loaded bullets into a machine gun, but another soldier had done the actual shooting. And so it went on, many of the soldiers denied any participation in the atrocities at all; some denied ever being at Oradour. But enough information was gleaned by the court to be able to establish the more significant details of what had actually occurred.

The time eventually came for the surviving victims of Oradour to give their evidence. The brothers Maurice and Joseph Beaubreuil gave details of the SS rounding-up the people in Le Champs de Foire. Hubert Desourteaux, although clearly in a state of mental anguish, was able to relate details of the executions that took place in his garage workshop. The survivors of the Laudy barn, Robert Hébras, Jean-Marcel Darthout, Yvon Roby, Clement Broussaudier and Mathieu Borie, told the court of their ordeal and their miraculous escape. They went on to relate the horrific details of how sixty men and boys had been machine-gunned, asphyxiated and burned alive.

One at a time, the other survivors such as Armand Senon and Paul Doutre and many of the local residents were able to tell the court their individual stories; most had lost some or all of their family during the massacre. Roger Godfrin, now a strapping teenager of sixteen, calmly related his tragic, but inspirational story in great detail ... the plucky child had become a fine young man and an excellent witness.

A frail but determined Marguerite Rouffange told the court of what had happened in the church. She was clearly unwell and the ordeal of having to recall the terror, the physical pain and injuries and the horror of witnessing the murders of her daughters and grandchild, was overwhelming; her husband Simon and their son, Jean, had also been murdered by the SS in one of the village barns. But despite all of this, this remarkable woman related her whole story to the court, in every detail.

Eventually, Judge Nussy Saint-Saëns and his six military presiding officers, retired from the courtroom to deliberate their verdicts' and to apportion punishments ... but even as they did so, the political divisions that had arisen between the peoples of northern and southern France as a result of the trial, had escalated to serious proportions.

Photographs and Illustrations

28.

*Inside the Church of Saint Martin today - I have not included the 1944 photographs which show horrific details of the massacre of the women and children inside the church*

*29. The Norman window from which Marguerite Rouffange escaped - Note the distorted iron mesh cover*

*30. The Confessional - Unharmed by the flames, but it holds a terrible secret*

*31.*

*Bullet holes in the War Memorial plaque*

*32. Le Champs de Foire - 'Doctor Jacque Desourteaux's car'*

*33. Madame Laudy's barn - The entrance where the SS set up their heavy machine guns*

Photographs and Illustrations

*34. Rabbit hutches - The temporary refuge of the survivors of the Laudy barn*

*35. A posy of little red flowers recently placed at the bakery ovens*

*36. Survivors: Armand Senon (left), Mathieu Borie (2nd left), Yvon Roby (4th Left), Jean-Marcel Darthout (glasses), Maurice & Joseph Beaubreuil (6th & 7th left), Hubert Desouteaux (5th right), Paul Doutre (2nd right), Clement Broussaudier (front centre) and Little Roger Godfrin (centre)*

*37.*

*Young mechanic Robert Hébras, survivor of the Laudy barn*

*38.*

*Marguerite Rouffange was the only survivor from the church*

*39. The church bell was melted beyond recognition*

*40. Church officials and volunteers recovering the dead*

*41. A sombre General Charles de Gaulle visits Oradour on Sunday 4th March 1945.*

Photographs and Illustrations

42.
Bordeaux 1953 -
Judge Marcel Nussy
Saint-Saëns presides

43. Courtroom Chaos - Georges René Boos chooses to sit with the Germans

Photographs and Illustrations

44.

*Boos denies the murder of the infant in the bakery - Note the large cooking pan in the foreground*

45.

*Oberscharführer Karl Lenz - The senior SS soldier in court at Bordeaux*

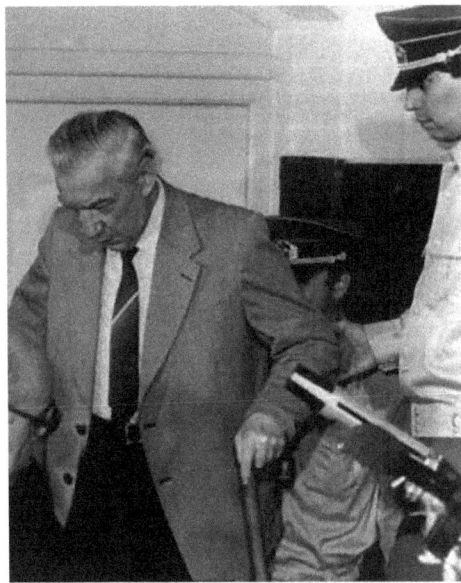

46.

*Untersturmführer Heinz Barth on trial in East Berlin in 1983*

47. *Witnesses 1983: Yvon Roby (2nd left), Jean-Marcel Darthout (3rd left), Maurice Beaubeuil (4th left) and Robert Hébras (right)*

Photographs and Illustrations

*48. Marguerite is now at rest in the village cemetery, near to her murdered love-ones*

*49. Within these two caskets are the remains of the 450 women, children and babies who perished in the church*

*50. Oradour-sur-Glane 2013 - Robert Hébras escorts President Gauck of Germany and President Hollande of France*

*51. Jean-Marcel Darthout and Robert Hébras remained life-long friends*

## Chapter 17

# Justice?

THE TRIAL OF THE GERMAN AND FRENCH SS soldiers in Bordeaux had caused massive political unrest throughout France. There had been large public demonstrations in the North of the country, particularly in the Alsace, the home of the *Malgré-nous* (the French-Alsatian soldiers who had been forced to act 'against their will'). It was seriously feared, and believed, that the people of the Alsace region might try to seek political-independence from France! But in the interest of national unity, much political appeasement was given to the Alsatians; even as the trial at Bordeaux was taking place, *new* laws were being quickly drafted to create amnesty for all Frenchmen who had been forcibly conscripted by the Germans. Inevitably, this 'retrospective legislation' was destined to have massive consequences for the survivors of Oradour and their families!

It was against the volatile background of national political unrest, that Judge Marcel Nussy Saint-Saëns was obliged to deliver the verdicts and sentences to the defendants at Bordeaux. Fearing that a violent demonstration might take place outside the courtroom, the judge decided to announce the verdicts during a night-time session. At 2.30am on Friday 13th February 1953, Nussy Saint-Saëns began his summing-up, which took over an hour, before delivering individual verdicts and punishments. None of the defendants were present ... they were to be notified of their individual fates later, within the confines of their prison cells. Based on the new laws of 'Collective Responsibility', the assumption of their guilt was a *'fait accompli'*.

Karl Lenz was found Guilty and given the Death sentence. He was the highest ranking soldier on trial and the Judges acted on the assumption that he must have participated in the massacre. Five of the other German soldiers were found Guilty and awarded terms of imprisonment varying from ten to twelve years. A seventh German was acquitted, as he was able to prove that he was not present at the massacre.

Georges René Boos was found Guilty and given the Death sentence. He was a Frenchman who had volunteered to join the SS and had attained promotion to the rank of sergeant; he was considered to be a traitor and he had admitted to the court that he had actively participated in the massacre. The other thirteen Frenchmen were all found Guilty and awarded terms of imprisonment varying from five to eight years.

Of the forty four ex-SS soldiers who were charged in their absence, all were given the Death sentence *'in absentia'*. This included General Heinz Lammerding, Captain Otto Khan and Second Lieutenant Heinz Barth. Field Marshal Hugo Sperrle, who had issued the infamous 'reprisal orders' was never charged with the crimes at Oradour; however, he had been previously indicted at Nuremberg for war major war crimes in 1945, but was found Not-Guilty due to lack of evidence! Coincidentally and perhaps fittingly, Sperrle died of natural causes just a few weeks after the trial at Bordeaux had ended.

## Chapter 17: Justice?

As expected, there was immediate political turmoil throughout France. The people in the southern regions, particularly the Limosan, considered the prison sentences to be ridiculously lenient ... conversely, the people in the Alsace were outraged that their 'sons' had been found Guilty! With the exception of Boos, the French SS soldiers, *'Malgré-nous'*, had been conscripted against their will and they had been forced to carry-out the killings at Oradour. The people of the Alsace considered them to be victims of the Nazis and the SS ... not the perpetrators of their crimes! In the northern French city of Strasbourg, war memorials were draped in black covers and public protests escalated!

But incredibly, within days, the new amnesty laws were enacted! Subsequently, the French SS soldiers were all pardoned and released ... with the exception of Boos, whose Death sentence was commuted to Life imprisonment! The public unrest in northern France, particularly in the Alsace and Lorraine regions, then rapidly de-escalated.

The German SS soldiers then protested that they too warranted the same clemency given to the Frenchmen; they also had been acting under a brutal and uncompromising disciplinary regime; their lives had been equally in peril if they had disobeyed the orders of their superiors! Within a few months, the German soldiers' prison sentences were radically reduced and they were permitted to return to their homes and families ... with the exception of Lenz, whose Death sentence was commuted to Life imprisonment.

As a consequence of the amnesties given to the Frenchmen, there followed much relief and celebration in the Alsace ... but for the survivors of Oradour-sur-Glane and their families, there was utter disbelief! Was there to be no justice for their murdered loved-ones? In the southern regions of France, particularly in the Limosan, there was public outrage. The names of the members of the French government who had voted for the amnesty laws, were publicly displayed at the entrance to the ruins of Oradour; black drapes were placed over the newly constructed memorial to the victims; Government officials were refused attendance to memorial ceremonies. The families of the victims, who had been granted France's highest award, the *Legion d'honneur*, returned it to the President! This unhappy predicament was destined to prevail throughout France for decades to come. To add to the grief and anger of the people of the Limosan, within five years, both Georges René Boos and Karl Lenz were released from prison to return to their homes and families!

## Chapter 18

# Barth

AFTER THE BITTER DISAPPOINTMENT OF THE TRIAL in Bordeaux, and the amnesties that followed, the survivors of the Oradour massacre had no choice but to again, settled down to their new lives as best they could. Decades passed, France and West Germany were now friends and allies. Bitter memories remained, but the peoples of the prosperous western European countries recognised the benefits of peace and reconciliation.

By the 1980s, in communist East Germany, there was a strong yearning to oust their Russian political masters and to re-unite with their countrymen in the capitalist free-West. As the East Germans gained confidence, the desire for greater political co-operation with the West increased; but this co-operation was not welcomed by all East Germans, particularly those former Nazis and SS soldiers who had committed war-crimes and were 'hiding in plain sight'. But the *will* to get rid of the Russians was gaining irreversible momentum! To seek further co-operation and credibility with Western Europe, the East German law-enforcement agencies became much more enthusiastic in apprehending war-criminals and bringing them to justice.

In the warm summer of 1981 at his home town of Gransee, deep within East Germany, Heinz Barth, the cruel Untersturmführer who had commanded the firing squads in Czechoslovakia and at Oradour-sur-Glane, was finally arrested for war-crimes. After a long and thorough investigation by the East German police, Barth was finally brought before a civilian court in East Berlin. Now sixty years of age, he had lived an ordinary and law abiding life and was in receipt of a war pension due to the loss of his leg during the fighting at Normandy. Barth had also become a proud husband, father and grandfather; but this did not deter the investigators; they were keen to show to the West that they were just as committed to bringing war-criminals to justice.

The East German police, in co-operation with the French and West German authorities, were able to put together a damning case against Barth. Over the previous decades, the combined law-enforcement agencies of Europe had accumulated an abundance of evidence relating to the massacre at Oradour-sur-Glane ... Barth, the only SS soldier of officer rank ever to stand trial for the massacre, was about to be confronted with the lot!

On a cold February morning in 1983, in the courtroom in East Berlin, Heinz Barth sat in the dock as the charges against him for war crimes were read out. Many of the survivors who had given evidence thirty years earlier at Bordeaux, again reiterated their stories; they included Robert Hébras, Jean-Marcel Darthout, Yvon Roby and Maurice Beaubreuil.

Barth, probably realising that the evidence against him was overwhelming, decided to tell the court the full details of his participation in the massacres in both Czechoslovakia and at Oradour-sur-Glane. He said that just prior to the Oradour massacre, he had been present at the meeting with Adolf Diekmann and Otto Khan in the hotel at Saint Junien. He went on to say that the decision to destroy the whole village and to execute the entire population was made by Diekmann during that meeting ... thereby confirming that the massacre at Oradour-sur-Glane had been entirely premeditated!

Barth also admitted to ordering his troops to carry out the executions of the men and boys in the Beaulieu forge and at Hubert Desourteaux's garage. He also gave details of the atrocities against the women and children in the church, but he always stuck to the standard SS excuse, 'I was obeying orders'. Inevitably, the court convicted Barth of all the charges and he was sentenced to Life imprisonment. He told the court that his only regret was that he was unlikely to see his grandchildren again!

## Chapter 19

# Aftermath

MARGUERITE ROUFFANGE LIVED A LONG LIFE; long enough to know justice had eventually caught up with Heinz Barth. She died peacefully in her bed in 1988 aged 90 years. She chose to be laid to rest in the old cemetery at Oradour, near to her murdered loved-ones. But Marguerite did *not* live long enough to learn that after 14 years imprisonment, Heinz Barth, was released on 'compassionate grounds' to enjoy the remainder of his life in comfort and freedom. Being a former soldier, he was permitted to continue to receive his war disability pension. He died peacefully at home in 2007.

Gruppenführer Heinz Lammerding, although condemned to Death *'in absentia'*, was never apprehended. In 1971 he died in prosperity and freedom at his home in Bad Tolz, West Germany, aged 65 years. Some 200 former SS soldiers attended his funeral.

In 1962, Hauptsturmführer Otto Khan was eventually traced to his home at Münster in West Germany, where he chose to make a written statement placing the blame for the massacre at Oradour entirely upon Diekmann. Despite being condemned to Death *'in absentia'* at Bordeaux, he was never extradited nor brought before any court for taking part in the massacre. Otto Eric Khan died peacefully at his home near Ottmarsbocholt, West Germany in 1977 aged 71 years.

Oberscharführer Karl Lenz, who had been incarcerated since the end of the war and subsequently sentenced to Death at Bordeaux in 1953, did not complete his commuted sentence of Life imprisonment. He was released in 1958, having served a total of thirteen years in custody.

Scharführer Georges René Boos, having been sentenced to Death at Bordeaux (later commuted to Life imprisonment) was released from prison just five years later in 1958. Returning to the Alsace region, he gained employment in the insurance business and lived a long and healthy life. He apparently chose to discontinue to use the French version of his forename, preferring to be known as Georg, (the German version). He died in the German border-town of Völklingen in 2015 aged 92 years.

After the war, the plucky refugee child Roger Godfrin, moved back to his native home town of Charly in the Lorraine region of northern France. In 1950 the town was renamed Charly-Oradour in memory of all the refugee families who had perished in the massacre. Roger died there in 2001 aged 65 years.

After the war, the Jewish refugees, Jaqueline, Francine and André Pinede, moved back to their home city of Bayonne in southern France. Jaqueline outlived her siblings and died there in 2017 aged 92 years.

Hubert Desourteaux never fully mentally recovered after witnessing the horrific murders of the men and boys in his garage workshop. He had also lost his parents and his three brothers in the massacre. He was able to give evidence at the trial in Bordeaux, but as he did so, it was clear that he remained in a state of mental trauma. Many years later, Hubert took his own life. He could perhaps be described as the very last victim of Oradour.

Survivors of the Laudy barn, Robert Hébras and Jean-Marcel Darthout, remained close friends for the remainder of their long lives. They regularly joined relatives and friends at the annual memorial ceremonies at Oradour. Jean-Marcel Darthout died peacefully aged 92 years. He rests in the old cemetery at Oradour-sur-Glane, near to the granite caskets that hold the remains of his wife Angéle, his mother and the other 450 women and children who perished in the church.

During his lifetime, Robert Hébras took great care to promote and preserve the memories of his family, friends and fellow villagers who had perished during the massacre at Oradour. He often escorted parties of students and school children around the ruins of the village. He became well-known throughout France and Western Europe for his work in promoting the memory of the victims of Oradour. He went on to host many of the Presidents of France and other international leaders during their visits to the village ... including, in 2013, President Joachim Gauck, the first German head of state to visit the village after the war. President Gauck chose the occasion to formally apologise on behalf of the German nation. In his later life, Robert received many awards, including the *Legion d'honneur*. In 2023 Robert Hébras, aged 97 years, died peacefully at his home in Saint Junien, just eight miles from Oradour.

All of the survivors of the massacre at Oradour are now gone. It was well into the twenty first century that war-crime investigators continued with their searches for former SS soldiers suspected of participating in the massacre. Between 2011 and 2014, the German police arrested seven elderly men suspected of involvement ...

Chapter 19: Aftermath

they were all in their mid-eighties, in poor health and were later released without charge.

The prospect of any further suspects being tried for the crimes at Oradour-sur-Glane are now extremely unlikely.

*52.*

*Oradour-sur-Glane: "Nobody lives here now."*
*350 homes and buildings destroyed*
*642 innocent men, women and children, murdered*

# Some Personal Thoughts

FROM TIME TO TIME I STILL ASK MYSELF THE question, 'what would you have done if you were in the same predicament as the young SS soldiers at Oradour?' I would like to think that I would have had the courage and the self-sacrifice to refuse to take part in the killings, and to encourage my fellow soldiers to do the same ... but I'm not certain that I would have been quite so noble or brave? I was brought up in a diverse and multi-cultural society which is largely peaceful, tolerant and compassionate. In contrast, Adolf Diekmann, Otto Khan and Heinz Barth had been institutionally conditioned since childhood to be brutal and cruel: the Hitler Youth; the Nazi 'Darwinian' survival of the fittest propaganda; the 'Euthanasia' programme to rid the country of invalids; the anti-Semitic 'Race Laws'; the excessively tough military training; their culture and education was based upon intolerance and Hate ... they knew little else!

Georges René Boos seems to have been a genuinely murderous bully who carried out his monstrous crimes with zeal. In my experience of the criminal world, people like Boos take whatever opportunities that arise to commit their perverted acts; I believe that he volunteered to join the SS in the full knowledge that such opportunities would inevitably come his way. Perhaps Boos was not entirely alone in the way that he had conducted himself at

Oradour? ... I suspect he was not!

What of the other SS soldiers, both Germans and Frenchmen? Yes, they participated in the massacre, albeit 'at pain of death'. But I suspect that they probably would not have done so if they had been given a choice? At least one soldier had the courage and compassion to permit the Jewish Pinede children to escape; he knew that he would have been severely punished, perhaps executed, if he had been found-out! ... I hope that I would have done the same?

During one of my many visits to Oradour, I found myself standing alone on the tram bridge. I had arrived quite early on a cold and windy spring morning. It was teeming with rain and I realised that I was probably the only person on the site. My wife Elaine and our friends, Jim and Hazel, had decided to leave me there for the day, whilst they sensibly pursued a nice warm breakfast in the nearby supermarket.

I had recently purchased a new camera and I was determined to take lots of photographs ... but as I stood there with my camera strapped around my neck and looking very much like a tourist at a 'theme park', I felt rather crass and intrusive. I was completely alone, but it just didn't feel right? I tucked my new camera under my waterproofed jacket and kept it out of site; there were plenty of photographs in the museum shop, where I later purchased an abundance of books and other publications for my personal interest.

As I stood on the bridge, I tried to imagine the SS convoy paused there ... Adolf Diekmann at the 'head', awaiting confirmation that the village was 'sealed-off' ... before thundering up to Le Champs de Foire to commence his monstrous crimes. To my right was the water mill and the riverbank, where little Roger Godfrin had hidden after being shot at by the SS guards. I followed the tramlines up the slight incline and into the village; to my right, almost completely concealed in the undergrowth, were the ruins of the Boucholle barn, the first of the execution sites ... every man and boy perished there! A little further along, I found the Milord Hotel storehouse ... again, nobody survived.

I walked into the church; it was completely deserted. I forced myself to envisage the soldiers lighting the fuse to their box of toxic explosives; the choking, terrified children. I stared at the shattered marble altar and the hundreds of bullet holes in the scorched and blackened walls. I noticed that the SS had specifically aimed their machine guns at the memorial plaque, which listed the names of the young men of the village who had lost their lives fighting for France during the Great War. I saw the wooden confessional, untouched by the flames, and the distorted, melted bronze bell that lay on the church floor. Above me were the three Norman windows ... the protective iron mesh twisted and misshapen by Marguerite Rouffange's frantic, super-human battle to survive.

As I walked further up the high street, to my left was Hubert Desourteaux's garage workshop; there I saw the little round holes blasted into the brickwork at knee-height? I had been previously informed that the reason the soldiers had 'aimed-low' was to maim their victims to prevent them fleeing ... before finishing them off with a second burst of gunfire. I recalled that Georges René Boos had admitted at his trial, that he had 'participated' in the executions in this garage, stating that he had done so on the direct orders of Otto Khan.

Facing the workshop, just across the high street, was Léopold Boucholle's bakery. My eyes were drawn towards the oven doors, where I noticed that someone had recently placed a 'posy' of crimson flowers ... the reality of the evil that had taken place in the bakery hit me hard. I am not prone to displaying my emotions, particularly in public, but I was overwhelmed with sadness and anger. I was grateful that the weather was foul and the site was deserted; it gave me the opportunity to shed an unstoppable tear in dignified solitude. It was at the bakery that I took my one and only photograph that day ... not a very good one as it turned out; but I am glad that I did; those little red flowers have become my personal 'memento' of Oradour.

I then made my way to the top of Le Rue Emile Desourteaux, where I found the remnants of the Post Office, and Monsieur Dupic's house, where the soldiers had feasted and drank wine whilst the village burned. I then walked back down the high street, passing the tram station and the Hotel Avril, where the Jewish Pinede family and the Alsatian Godfrin family had resided. Next door were the ruins of the Hébras house; the abode of the young mechanic Robert, who had miraculously survived being burned alive in the Laudy barn.

I moved on to Monsieur Denis's wine storeroom, another mass execution site; nobody survived. Continuing down, I stopped at the Beaulieu forge, where yet more men and boys were gunned down and burned; it was also the place where the unfortunate group of touring cyclists were lined-up and shot.

I then ventured into the open space of the village green: Le Champs de Foire; this is where Diekmann, Khan, Barth, Boos, their SS troops and French conscripts rounded-up the villagers and the refugee families and their city visitors ... and then marched them off to their agonising deaths in the pre-ordained execution sites. Doctor Jacques Desourteaux's Citroen *Berline* remained rusting away on the corner of the green. I have since learned that this was probably not his car, but it is retained there as a symbol of his fateful return to the village that day. At the opposite corner of Le Champs de Foire, I discovered the home of Armand Senon, the feisty footballer with the broken leg: a courageous and miraculous survivor.

I then walked the short distance to the ruins of the Laudy barn; I saw the little wooden door at the back where Robert Hébras, Jean-Marcel Darthout, Clement Broussaudier, Yvon Roby, Henri Poutaraud and the stone mason Mathieu Borie, began their escape from the raging smoke and fire. Nearby were the smoke-blackened rabbit hutches where they had hidden. I traced their escape route to the cemetery pathway; there I discovered the place where Henri Poutaraud was gunned-down as he desperately tried to escape the inferno.

I continued to brave the unrelenting rainfall as I roamed solitarily around the ruins. I spent the whole day there, wandering around in deep contemplation ... and perhaps slight confusion? Why was I actually there? Had I fallen into the trap of merely being 'morbidly curious'? I hoped not! But tragic and atrocious though it was, it had all happened such a long time ago! Nonetheless, the personal message that I got from my visit was: 'Please God, don't ever let this happen again!'

As I have stated earlier, the stark ruins of Oradour-sur-Glane are slowly 'weathering'. It is a vast site and maintaining its crumbling structures must be getting more and more difficult. Many people believe that the time has come for the village to be rebuilt and re-inhabited, perhaps with the exception of the Church of Saint Martin, which they say should remain as a permanent memorial to the massacre? I have mixed thoughts; but such decisions, quite rightly, are the prerogative of the people of France, particularly the decedents of the victims and survivors. I am personally appreciative that General de Gaulle had the foresight to preserve the village; and I am certain that the site has proven to be an inspirational and appropriate memorial to the victims. It is also, of course, a formidable warning to the leaders and the peoples of the World ... 'This is what can happen when the peace breaks-down and mankind becomes bestial'!

I am not sure that I have learned any of the answers as to why soldiers sometimes become 'monsters'? Perhaps the reality is that *many* of us are capable of bestial behaviour, but are deterred by from acting as such by the laws and punishments of our societies? Sadly, I am aware that, even in our modern, largely peaceful society, many people are prone to violently react to the most menial provocation. A trivial, but very common, modern example of such behaviour is 'road rage'; I have experienced it both professionally and personally and I dread to think what the consequences would have been if I had actually carried-out some of the violent thoughts that I have experienced on such occasions?

Of course, it is silly to compare the trivialities of everyday 'squabbles' with the extreme mental and physical pressures that soldiers *must* endure during warfare. When we become soldiers, we are trained, conditioned and equipped with a formidable range of weaponry, designed to kill our enemies quickly and efficiently. When a soldier, for whatever reason, loses mental control of his or her actions, the consequences are potentially vast and devastating! Perhaps it is therefore inevitable that people like Adolf Diekmann, Otto Khan, Heinz Barth and Georges René Boos will, given the opportunity, resort to their naturally 'monstrous' instincts? Warfare and the breakdown of law and order, inevitably presents potentially violent criminals with opportunities that they probably would not experience during peacetime. When peace finally came to Europe in 1945, many of the murderous soldiers who had participated in the massacre at Oradour, simply 'blended' back to normality, happily returning to their families and becoming good law-abiding citizens for the remainder of their lives.

It is now the autumn of 2023, and nearly eighty years have passed since the SS soldiers murdered the villagers of Oradour-sur-Glane. The world has changed! Education and science have made it a wonderful world, we eat well, we live longer … but sadly, mankind continues to fight wars. I am sat in my armchair at home enjoying a cup of coffee and a slice of toast. I am watching the morning BBC television news … some heavily-armed *soldiers* have attacked a music festival being held in a small peaceful Israeli town near to Gaza … in just a few short hours they have destroyed family homes, abducted hostages … and sadistically butchered over a thousand civilians … innocent men, women, children and babies …

# Acknowledgements

I BEGIN BY EXTENDING MY THANKS TO OUR LONG-suffering friends, Jim and Hazel McCarthy, who not only *found* Oradour for me, but taxied me all over the rolling countryside of the Limosan ... several times! My thanks go to my friend Peter Jones, a retired policeman, who interrupted his well-earned holiday in the USA to track-down one or two important publications! My thanks also go to my professional colleague, retired Detective Sergeant Ian Osbourne, who provided me with a key publication about the SS Das Reich division, which he found at a car boot sale! Thank you to my sister Pauline and my nephew Justin, for their administrative support and encouragement. I express my love and gratitude to my wife Elaine for putting up with all the upheaval and travel around central France! A big thank you goes to my cousin *Petesie*, better known as the writer and poet Tom Balch, for his soulful and soldierly poems. I am in awe of the heroism and sacrifices of my dad, Sergeant George Haines and my grandad, Private Ernest Lewis, survivors-both, of the two World Wars. Finally, my blessing goes to the soldiers, past and present of all nations, who have fought with honour and humanity.

# Photographs and Illustrations

1. Oradour Soldiers of Shame by Roy Haines *(Front Cover)*
2. Oradour-sur-Glane – In better times *(Maryanik Gaultier)*
3. Rue Emile Desourteaux today *(Roy Haines)*
4. The boucherie in the high street *(Marie Parker)*
5. A 'sad-faced' old car gazes across the High Street *(Marie Parker)*
6. Hubert Desourteaux's garage workshop – Bullet holes at knee-height *(Marie Parker)*
7. Petrol rationing – Most of the villager's cars were stored in lock-ups for the duration of the war *(Marie Parker)*
8. The excitable Kaiser Wilhelm II
9. Adolf Hitler – Another psychologically unbalanced leader
10. Vichy President Phillippe Petain and his Nazi puppet-master
11. 'Dealing with the opposition' *(Sir David Low, Evening Standard c.1934)*
12. Heinrich Himmler – SS Reichführer
13. Reinhard Heydrich – Mastermind of the Holocaust
14. June 6th 1944 Normandy – Operation 'Overlord' the Allied Invasion *(US Library of Congress)*
15. Petain's 'La Milice' round-up their fellow countrymen
16. Tulle – An SS officer's sketch of the hangings

17. Captured SS officer Sturmbannführer Helmut Kämpfe
18. The Church of Saint Martin before the massacre
19. The 'other' Oradour – A recent image of Oradour-sur-Vayres *(Roy Haines)*
20. The local Resistance Leader Georges Guingouin, who ordered the execution of Sturmbannführer Helmut Kämpfe
21. Violette Szabó, George Cross – The courageous SOE agent
22. The pompous Field Marshal Hugo Sperrle – Author of the 'reprisal orders'
23. Gruppenführer Heinz Lammerding – Das Reich division commander
24. The 'monstrous' Sturmbannführer Adolf Diekmann, who planned and executed the massacre
25. Experienced killers – Untersturmführer Heinz Barth and Hauptsturmführer Otto Khan
26. The Hotel De La Gare in Saint Junien, where Diekmann planned the massacre *(Roy Haines)*
27. A Map of Oradour-sur-Glane *(Roy Haines)*
28. Inside the Church of Saint Martin today
29. The Norman window from which Marguerite Rouffange escaped
30. The Confessional – Unharmed by the flames *(Marie Parker)*
31. Bullet holes in the War Memorial plaque *(Marie Parker)*
32. Le Champs de Foire – 'Doctor Jacque Desourteaux's car' *(Marie Parker)*
33. Madame Laudy's barn *(Marie Parker)*
34. The rabbit hutches *(Marie Parker)*

35. The bakery ovens *(Roy Haines)*
36. Survivors
37. Young mechanic Robert Hébras
38. Marguerite Rouffange was the only survivor from the church
39. The church bell was melted beyond recognition *(Marie Parker)*
40. Church officials and volunteers recovering the dead
41. General Charles de Gaulle – Sunday 4th March 1945
42. Bordeaux 1953 – Judge Marcel Nussy Saint-Saëns presides
43. Courtroom Chaos
44. Boos denies the murder of the infant in the bakery
45. Oberscharführer Karl Lenz – The senior SS soldier in court at Bordeaux
46. Untersturmführer Heinz Barth on trial in East Berlin in 1983
47. Witnesses 1983
48. Marguerite is now at rest in the village cemetery *(Marie Parker)*
49. Within these two caskets are the remains of the 450 women, children and babies who perished in the church *(Marie Parker)*
50. Oradour 2013 – Robert Hébras escorts Presidents Gauck and Hollande
51. Jean-Marcel Darthout and Robert Hébras
52. Oradour-sur-Glane – "Nobody lives here now"
53. The Author *(Back Page)*

# Bibliography

Jens Kruuse
*Madness at Oradour*, 1969

Philp Beck
*Oradour – Village of the Dead*, 1979

Max Hastings
*Das Reich*, 1981

Otto Weidinger
*Das Reich 1943-45*, 1991

Guy Pauchou & Dr Pierre Masfrand
*Oradour-sur-Glane: A Vision of Horror*, 1993 edition

Pascal Maysounave
*Oradour – Plus Prés De La Vérité*, 1996

André Desourteaux &, Robert Hébras
*Oradour/Glane: Notre Village Assassiné*, 1998

Sara Farmer
*Martyred Village*, 1999

Philip Beck
*Oradour – The Massacre and Aftermath*, 2004

Jean-Jacques Fouché
*Massacre at Oradour – France 1944*, 2005

Douglas W. Hawes
*Oradour – The Final Verdict*, 2007

# Other Reading

Robin Mackness
*Oradour – Massacre & Aftermath*, 1988

Helen Watts
*One Day In Oradour*, 2013

# The Author

ROY HAINES SERVED AS A SOLDIER FOR SIX YEARS, operating landing craft and fast launches on military deployments throughout Europe and the Middle East. He views his brief military service as a significant foundation to his long and eventful policing career. As a Ministry of Defence police inspector, Roy was involved in hundreds of criminal enquiries and policing operations throughout the UK and Northern Ireland. During the final years of his service he was temporarily promoted to chief inspector and was responsible for planning major maritime and firearms operations. Roy is now retired and is a keen history buff. He and his wife Elaine live on the south coast of England, joyously spending their time with their son Martin, daughter Marie and their four grandchildren.

www.ingramcontent.com/pod-product-compliance
Lightning Source LLC
Chambersburg PA
CBHW061406160426
42813CB00088B/2711